Mandawa : The Intersection Of Art, Culture, And Architecture In Rajasthan

By

Dr. Akshay Anil Wayal

Dr. Shobhan Sadhan Kelkar

Dr. Ajinkya Pradeep Niphadkar

2025

Copyright

Mandawa: The Intersection of Art, Culture, and Architecture in Rajasthan
© 2025 Dr. Akshay Anil Wayal, Dr. Shobhan Sadhan Kelkar, Dr. Ajinkya Pradeep Niphadkar

This book is a work of original research and documentation. Every effort has been made to credit all sources appropriately. Any errors or omissions are unintentional and will be corrected in subsequent editions.

For permissions, inquiries, or feedback, contact: akshaywayal69@gmail.com

First Edition, 2025
Printed in India

Dedication

This book is dedicated to all those who have inspired, supported, and guided us throughout our journey in exploring the rich heritage of Mandawa, Rajasthan.

To our beloved family, whose unwavering encouragement and belief in our vision have been the foundation of our endeavors. Their love and support have carried are through every challenge and fueled our passion for uncovering the stories of art, culture, and architecture.

To our mentors and teachers, who instilled in me the values of curiosity, dedication, and respect for knowledge. Their guidance has shaped our academic pursuits and inspired us to contribute meaningfully to the study of heritage and preservation.

To the people of Mandawa, whose traditions, creativity, and resilience are embedded in the havelis, frescoes, and streets of this remarkable town. Their connection to their history and their efforts to keep it alive have been a profound source of inspiration.

To the artists, architects, and craftsmen of the past, whose vision and skill turned Mandawa into a living museum of art and design. This work is a tribute to their enduring legacy and a call to appreciate and protect their contributions for generations to come.

Finally, to all readers, scholars, and enthusiasts of art and culture, We dedicate this book with the hope that it will ignite a deeper appreciation for the beauty and significance of preserving our shared heritage. May it inspire you to see the world through the lens of history, creativity, and cultural pride.

With gratitude and humility,
Dr. Akshay Anil Wayal

Dr. Shobhan Sadhan Kelkar

Dr. Ajinkya Pradeep Niphadkar

Table of Contents

Preface

Rajasthan, the land of kings and warriors, is renowned for its vibrant history, rich cultural heritage, and breathtaking architecture. In the heart of this storied landscape lies Mandawa, a town that embodies the essence of Rajasthan's artistic, cultural, and architectural legacy. Known as the "Open-Air Art Gallery," Mandawa offers a vivid canvas where centuries-old traditions continue to thrive amidst the marvels of frescoed havelis, ornate temples, and palatial forts.

This book, *Mandawa: The Intersection of Art, Culture, and Architecture in Rajasthan*, invites readers to embark on a journey through this charming town, uncovering the intricate tapestry woven by the many influences that have shaped it over time. Mandawa's unique architectural style reflects a fusion of Rajput, Mughal, and Marwari traditions, infused with local artistry and craftsmanship, providing a glimpse into the lives of its erstwhile aristocracy.

As we traverse the narrow lanes and expansive courtyards of Mandawa, we discover not just the beauty of its frescoes and wall paintings but also the deep cultural significance embedded within them. These works of art are more than just decorative elements; they are windows into the region's history, folklore, mythology, and values. From the intricate depictions of royal life to the colorful portrayals of daily routines, the art of Mandawa reflects the intersection of time, place, and identity.

The architecture of Mandawa is a testament to the enduring ingenuity and creativity of its people. The grand havelis, with their ornately carved wooden facades and meticulously painted walls, stand as symbols of both aesthetic grandeur and the social structure of the time. They reveal how architecture in Rajasthan was not just a reflection of power, but also an expression of the cultural ethos, the blending of form and function.

This book aims to capture the essence of Mandawa through the lens of art, culture, and architecture, offering both a historical account and a visual journey. The intersection of these elements in Mandawa provides a unique narrative of Rajasthan's rich past, showcasing how these artistic and architectural traditions continue to influence the region's identity today. Whether you are an art enthusiast, a history lover, or simply someone with a passion for discovering new places, Mandawa offers an unparalleled glimpse into the soul of Rajasthan.

Through this exploration, we hope to inspire a deeper appreciation for Mandawa's vibrant heritage, inviting future generations to preserve and celebrate the beauty that lies at the crossroads of art, culture, and architecture.

1.INTRODUCTION

Mandawa, a small yet historically rich town in the Shekhawati region of Rajasthan, stands as a magnificent repository of art, culture, and history. Known as an "open-air art gallery," Mandawa is adorned with exquisite frescoes, grand havelis, and a regal fort that echo tales of its glorious past. The town, though modest in size, has been a canvas where stories of trade, royalty, and artistic brilliance were painted over centuries. Mandawa's history, steeped in the legacy of its rulers and the ingenuity of its merchants, provides a fascinating glimpse into a bygone era that continues to captivate visitors today.

The story of Mandawa begins in the mid-18th century when it was established by Thakur Nawal Singh, a prominent figure of the Shekhawat Rajputs. The Shekhawats were descendants of Rao Shekha, a legendary 15th-century Rajput chieftain who laid the foundation of the Shekhawati region. With their stronghold in the arid expanse of northeastern Rajasthan, the Shekhawats were known for their valor, administrative prowess, and cultural patronage. It was Thakur Nawal Singh's vision that turned Mandawa into a fortified settlement, strategically located along ancient trade routes that connected the Indian subcontinent with Central Asia, Persia, and the Middle East.

Trade was the lifeblood of Mandawa during its formative years. Caravans laden with textiles, spices, precious metals, and other commodities crisscrossed through the town, making it a bustling hub of commerce. The wealth generated from this trade brought prosperity to Mandawa and enabled the local elite, particularly the merchant class, to invest in grand architectural and artistic endeavors. The town became a testament to the opulence and sophistication of the Shekhawati merchants, who sought to showcase their success through magnificent havelis adorned with intricate frescoes.

At the heart of Mandawa's history lies its majestic fort, built in 1755 by Thakur Nawal Singh. Serving as both a defensive structure and a residence, the fort was designed to reflect the grandeur and strength of the Shekhawat dynasty. Constructed with a blend of Rajput and Mughal architectural styles, the fort boasted imposing gates, intricately carved balconies, and richly decorated interiors. The fort became the nucleus of the town, around which Mandawa developed into a thriving settlement. Today, the Mandawa Fort has been transformed into a heritage hotel, allowing visitors to immerse themselves in the regal ambiance of its historic halls and courtyards.

While the fort stands as a symbol of Mandawa's royal heritage, the town's true artistic legacy is enshrined in its havelis. These traditional mansions, built between the 18th and 20th centuries, are masterpieces of craftsmanship. The havelis were constructed by wealthy merchants who spared no expense in making their homes both functional and aesthetically extraordinary. The walls of these havelis became canvases for vibrant frescoes, painted using natural pigments derived from minerals, plants, and other organic materials.

The frescoes of Mandawa are an unparalleled artistic achievement. They depict a rich tapestry of themes, ranging from mythological tales of Hindu deities like Krishna and Shiva to scenes of royal courts, folklore, and even glimpses of daily life. As the region came into contact with colonial influences in the 19th century, the frescoes began to incorporate modern motifs, such as depictions of British officials, steam engines, and aeroplanes. This blending of traditional and contemporary themes reflects the dynamic cultural and economic environment of Mandawa during this period.

Beyond its architecture and art, Mandawa's history is also shaped by the people who called it home. The Shekhawati merchants, renowned for their business acumen, played a crucial role in the town's development. These entrepreneurial families amassed great wealth through trade and often migrated to larger cities like Calcutta, Bombay, and Delhi to expand their ventures. However, they maintained strong ties to their roots in Mandawa, channeling their wealth into the construction of havelis, temples, and wells, leaving behind an indelible mark on the town's landscape.

In the 20th century, as trade routes shifted and modern infrastructure developed, Mandawa, like many other towns in the Shekhawati region, experienced a decline in its economic prominence. Many merchant families left the town, and their grand havelis were gradually abandoned. Yet, even in this state of partial neglect, Mandawa's charm and historical significance endured. The intricate frescoes, though weathered by time, remained a testament to the artistic brilliance of the Shekhawati artisans.

Today, Mandawa has emerged as a prominent tourist destination, attracting visitors from around the world who come to marvel at its architectural and artistic treasures. Heritage hotels like the Mandawa Fort offer a glimpse into the royal lifestyle, while guided tours of the town's havelis provide a deeper understanding of its rich cultural and historical context. The annual Shekhawati Festival further showcases the vibrant traditions of the region, celebrating its music, dance, and art forms.

Mandawa's history is a tale of transformation and resilience. From its origins as a fortified trade outpost to its heyday as a center of art and commerce, the town has witnessed centuries of change while preserving its unique identity. Its frescoes, havelis, and fort stand as timeless monuments to the vision and creativity of its people. For those who visit Mandawa, the town offers not just a journey through history but an unforgettable experience of the grandeur and grace that define Rajasthan's cultural heritage.

1.1 Origins of Mandawa

The origins of Mandawa are rooted in the rich history of the Shekhawati region in Rajasthan, a land known for its valor, artistry, and vibrant cultural legacy. Mandawa, a jewel of this region, was established in the mid-18th century during a period of strategic expansion and consolidation by the Shekhawat Rajputs. This influential clan, descendants of the 15th-century chieftain Rao Shekha, played a pivotal role in shaping the political and cultural landscape of northeastern Rajasthan.

Thakur Nawal Singh, a prominent Shekhawat leader, is credited with founding Mandawa around 1755. The establishment of the town was driven by both strategic necessity and economic foresight. At the time, the Shekhawati region was a crucial link along the ancient caravan trade routes that connected India with Central Asia, Persia, and the Middle East. These routes were bustling with merchants transporting goods like textiles, spices, and precious metals. Recognizing the importance of controlling and protecting this lucrative trade network, Nawal Singh established Mandawa as a fortified settlement.

The Mandawa Fort, built under Thakur Nawal Singh's direction, became the centerpiece of the town's origins. Designed with a blend of Rajput and Mughal architectural elements, the fort was both a defensive stronghold and a symbol of power. Its high walls, intricately carved gateways, and ornate interiors reflected the prestige of the Shekhawat rulers while providing security against potential invaders and bandits that often threatened trade caravans. The fort also served as a residence and administrative center, fostering the growth of a thriving community around it.

As Mandawa developed, it began to attract traders and artisans seeking opportunities in this bustling hub. The town's strategic location and the security offered by the Shekhawats made it an ideal base for merchants, who brought with them not only their wealth but also their culture and traditions. Over time, Mandawa grew from a modest fortified settlement into a vibrant trading post, its prosperity fueled by the steady flow of goods and people passing through its gates.

The Shekhawati merchants, known for their entrepreneurial spirit, played a significant role in Mandawa's early growth. These merchants were not just traders but also patrons of art and architecture, laying the foundation for the town's future as a cultural and artistic hub. They invested their wealth in constructing grand havelis, adorned with intricate frescoes that depicted mythological tales, folklore, and scenes from daily life. This architectural tradition would later define Mandawa's identity as a center of artistic excellence.

Thus, the origins of Mandawa are deeply intertwined with the Shekhawat dynasty's vision and the entrepreneurial energy of its merchant class. What began as a strategic outpost grew into a flourishing town that not only safeguarded trade routes but also became a beacon of art and culture. Today, the foundations laid by Thakur Nawal Singh and the Shekhawati merchants continue to echo in Mandawa's timeless frescoes, majestic fort, and enduring charm.

1.2 The Shekhawati Region and Its Legacy

Mandawa is part of the larger Shekhawati region, which comprises several towns and villages known for their rich cultural and artistic heritage. Named after Rao Shekha, who established his rule in the 15th century, the region flourished under the patronage of the Shekhawat rulers. Their legacy is evident in the magnificent forts, temples, and havelis adorned with intricate frescoes and murals.

The Shekhawati region has a unique place in history as a center of both trade and artistry. The wealth accumulated by its merchants, coupled with the royal patronage of art and architecture, created an environment where creativity thrived. Mandawa, as one of the region's gems, reflects this legacy in its grandiose structures and vibrant cultural expressions.

2. MANDAWA UNDER RAJPUT RULE

Mandawa, a picturesque town in Rajasthan's Shekhawati region, flourished under the rule of the Rajputs, particularly the Shekhawat clan. This period marked an era of strategic foresight, architectural grandeur, and cultural prosperity that laid the foundation for Mandawa's lasting legacy. Governed by the Shekhawat Rajputs, the town emerged as a fortified settlement and a thriving hub of trade and artistry, with its rulers playing a pivotal role in shaping its identity as a cultural and historical landmark.

The Shekhawat Rajputs, descendants of Rao Shekha, established their dominion over the Shekhawati region in the 15th century. Known for their martial prowess and administrative acumen, the Shekhawats carved out a legacy of resilience and creativity in the arid lands of northeastern Rajasthan. Mandawa became an integral part of this heritage during the mid-18th century when it was founded by Thakur Nawal Singh, a visionary leader of the Shekhawat clan.

The establishment of Mandawa under Rajput rule was driven by both strategic and economic considerations. Positioned along vital trade routes that connected India with Central Asia, Persia, and the Middle East, Mandawa was ideally located to serve as a trade and security outpost. The Rajputs, adept at fortifying their territories, constructed the Mandawa Fort as a defensive bastion to safeguard the town and the caravans that passed through it. Built in 1755, the fort reflected the architectural brilliance of the Shekhawats, with its imposing walls, intricately designed gateways, and richly adorned interiors. It became the focal point of Mandawa's development, both as a stronghold of Rajput authority and as a nucleus around which the town flourished.

Rajput rule in Mandawa was marked by the Shekhawats' commitment to fostering trade and commerce. The town's secure environment attracted merchants from across the region, who sought to capitalize on its strategic location and protection. The Shekhawat rulers encouraged these traders by offering patronage and ensuring the safety of their goods. This mutually beneficial relationship led to the economic prosperity of Mandawa, enabling it to grow into a bustling trading hub.

The wealth generated through trade under Rajput rule had a profound impact on Mandawa's cultural and architectural landscape. The Shekhawat rulers, known for their patronage of art and architecture, set the tone for the town's artistic development. They commissioned grand structures, including temples and palaces, that showcased a blend of Rajput and Mughal influences. Their legacy of architectural patronage inspired the wealthy merchant class to construct havelis that would become the hallmark of Mandawa's identity.

Mandawa's havelis, built during the Shekhawat period, were not just residences but also symbols of prestige and prosperity. These grand mansions, adorned with intricate frescoes, reflected the artistic sensibilities of the time. The frescoes depicted a variety of themes, including Hindu mythology, historical events, and scenes from daily life. They also incorporated elements of modernity, such as depictions of trains, steamships, and colonial influences, highlighting the dynamic interplay between tradition and innovation during Rajput rule.

Under the Shekhawat Rajputs, Mandawa also became a center for cultural preservation and expression. Festivals, music, and dance flourished in the town, creating a vibrant social milieu that celebrated Rajput traditions and values. The rulers upheld the warrior ethos of their lineage, organizing jousts, hunting expeditions, and ceremonial processions that showcased their martial heritage. At the same time, they nurtured a spirit of inclusivity, fostering a diverse community of traders, artisans, and scholars who contributed to Mandawa's cultural fabric.

The Shekhawat rulers' governance extended beyond economic and cultural development. They were known for their administrative efficiency and efforts to improve the lives of their subjects. They constructed wells, stepwells, and water reservoirs to address the challenges of the region's arid climate. These infrastructural initiatives not only supported agricultural activities but also ensured the well-being of the local population, cementing the Shekhawats' reputation as benevolent rulers.

Despite its prosperity, Mandawa under Rajput rule was not without challenges. The region's strategic importance made it a target for rival factions and invaders. However, the Shekhawat rulers' military expertise and the fortifications they established ensured the town's resilience. Mandawa's fort became a symbol of defiance and strength, standing as a testament to the Shekhawat Rajputs' ability to protect their territory and people.

As the 19th century unfolded, Mandawa, like the rest of Shekhawati, faced the winds of change brought about by British colonial influence. While the Shekhawat rulers retained a degree of autonomy, the shifting dynamics of power and trade began to reshape the region. Many of Mandawa's merchant families migrated to larger cities, seeking new opportunities in emerging industries. Despite these changes, the legacy of Rajput rule remained etched in the town's architectural and cultural heritage.

Today, Mandawa stands as a living museum of its Rajput past. The fort, havelis, and frescoes that define the town are enduring reminders of the Shekhawat rulers' vision and contributions. The traditions of artistry, hospitality, and resilience that flourished under Rajput rule continue to inspire Mandawa's identity, attracting visitors from around the world who come to experience its timeless charm.

The history of Mandawa under Rajput rule is a story of foresight, creativity, and determination. It reflects the Shekhawats' ability to transform a desert town into a flourishing hub of trade, art, and culture, leaving behind a legacy that continues to resonate across generations.

2.1 The Rise of the Marwari Merchants

The rise of the Marwari merchants is a story of extraordinary ambition, resilience, and entrepreneurial ingenuity. Emerging from the arid landscapes of Rajasthan, particularly the Shekhawati region, the Marwaris transformed themselves from local traders into a dominant business community in India and abroad. Over the centuries, they adapted to changing economic environments, navigated shifting political landscapes, and built networks that spanned continents. Their journey from humble beginnings to becoming a cornerstone of India's economic framework is a testament to their foresight, adaptability, and perseverance.

2.2 Origins in Rajasthan

The term "Marwari" derives from Marwar, a region in western Rajasthan, though it broadly includes people from Shekhawati and other parts of the state. Rajasthan's arid climate, limited agricultural potential, and resource scarcity forced its inhabitants to look beyond their homeland for economic opportunities. The Shekhawati region, home to towns like Mandawa, Nawalgarh, and Jhunjhunu, played a crucial role in the early history of Marwari traders. These towns were located along ancient trade routes, connecting India to Central Asia and the Middle East.

During the 18th century, the Shekhawati Rajput rulers, particularly the Shekhawat clan, provided a conducive environment for trade by ensuring safety for merchants and encouraging economic activities. These conditions allowed the Marwaris to emerge as intermediaries in the trade of textiles, spices, and precious metals. The wealth accumulated through these ventures enabled them to invest in local architecture, including grand havelis and temples that still stand as cultural landmarks.

2.3 Expansion Beyond Rajasthan

The Marwaris' rise began in earnest when they migrated from their homeland to other parts of India in search of better economic prospects. By the 18th and 19th centuries, many Marwari families had settled in cities such as Calcutta (Kolkata), Bombay (Mumbai), and Madras (Chennai). These urban centers were becoming hubs of commerce and industry under British colonial rule, offering immense opportunities for growth.

In Calcutta, the Marwaris thrived by engaging in the lucrative jute trade, becoming key players in the production and export of jute goods. They also excelled in the textile and opium trade, leveraging their networks to establish themselves as indispensable intermediaries between Indian producers and British firms. Their migration was not just physical but also economic—they brought with them a tradition of astute financial management and adaptability that allowed them to flourish in new environments.

2.4 Attributes of Success

The Marwari merchants' rise can be attributed to a combination of inherent qualities and learned skills:

1. **Adaptability**: The Marwaris displayed an exceptional ability to adapt to new markets and industries. Whether transitioning from rural trade to urban commerce or embracing colonial-era industrialization, they demonstrated remarkable flexibility.

2. **Community Networks**: Marwaris built strong intra-community networks based on trust and shared values. These networks provided them with access to credit, market information, and support in times of need, allowing them to operate efficiently and reduce risks.

3. **Frugality and Reinvestment**: Marwaris were known for their disciplined financial practices, including frugality and a focus on reinvesting profits into their businesses. This approach enabled sustained growth and diversification.

4. **Philanthropy and Social Ties**: The Marwaris maintained strong connections to their native towns through philanthropy. They built schools, hospitals, temples, and water reservoirs, earning goodwill and creating a sense of loyalty among their communities.

2.5 Colonial Era and Industrial Ventures

The British colonial era was a transformative period for the Marwaris. With the expansion of the British Empire, India's economy underwent significant changes, including the growth of industries such as textiles, jute, and tea. The Marwaris were quick to capitalize on these developments, transitioning from traditional trade to industrial ventures.

The Birlas, one of the most prominent Marwari families, exemplified this shift. Beginning as small traders, they ventured into jute manufacturing in the early 20th century and later diversified into cement, aluminum, and textiles. The Marwaris also played a vital role in the informal banking sector, using the hundi system to provide credit to traders and entrepreneurs. Their financial acumen positioned them as key players in India's industrial and commercial landscape.

2.6 Challenges and Adaptability

Despite their success, the Marwaris faced numerous challenges. The rise of competing business communities, colonial policies that favored British firms, and economic downturns tested their resilience. Additionally, their move into industries required them to navigate complex labor issues, government regulations, and volatile markets.

Nevertheless, the Marwaris adapted to these challenges with characteristic ingenuity. They leveraged their community networks to weather economic storms, diversified their investments to reduce risks, and maintained close ties with policymakers to safeguard their interests. Their ability to read market trends and anticipate changes allowed them to stay ahead of their competitors.

2.7 Post-Independence Era

India's independence in 1947 marked a new chapter in the Marwari story. As the country embarked on a path of industrialization and economic self-reliance, the Marwaris emerged as key contributors to this transformation. Families like the Birlas, Goenkas, and Poddars expanded their businesses into new sectors, including telecommunications, steel, and energy.

The Marwaris' emphasis on education and innovation enabled them to adapt to the demands of a modern economy. They also became prominent philanthropists, establishing universities, research institutes, and healthcare facilities that contributed to India's social and economic development.

2.8 Global Expansion

In the late 20th and early 21st centuries, the Marwaris extended their influence beyond India. They established businesses in Southeast Asia, Africa, and the Middle East, leveraging their networks and expertise to tap into global markets. At the same time, they maintained their cultural and philanthropic traditions, supporting their native towns and fostering a sense of community among the diaspora.

2.9 Legacy and Continuing Impact

The rise of the Marwari merchants is not just a story of economic success; it is a narrative of resilience, vision, and cultural pride. From their humble beginnings in Rajasthan's arid lands to becoming a global business community, the Marwaris have left an indelible mark on India's economic and cultural history.

Their legacy continues to inspire new generations of entrepreneurs, exemplifying the values of hard work, adaptability, and community support. The Marwari story is a powerful reminder of how vision and perseverance can overcome even the most challenging circumstances, creating opportunities not just for individual success but for the prosperity of entire communities.

Today, as India embraces globalization and innovation, the Marwaris remain at the forefront of its economic evolution, contributing to the nation's growth while honoring their rich heritage. Their story is a testament to the enduring power of entrepreneurship and the strength of human ambition.

2.10 Colonial Era and Decline of Mandawa

Mandawa which is situated in the dry and desert part of Shekhawati in Rajasthan, had already served as a commercial and cultural activity region even before the invasion of British colonial forces in India. The Shekhawat Rajputs who had constructed and ruled Mandawa were of great military and administrative repute and the town developed well under their administration. The town's prosperity was also due to trade, especially with Central Asia, Persia, and the Middle East. Such a trade was facilitated by the town's placement on vibrant trade routes transporting fabrics, spices, and opium throughout the region. Thus, Mandawa turned out to be buzzing with activity and attracted local as well as distant merchants. But when the British East India Company started tightening its grip over the Indian subcontinent in the late 18th century, Mandawa, like many other towns in the state of Rajasthan, suffered some indirect effects due to the changes in rule and the trade. Shekhawati was not conquered by British forces directly, but the British almost dominated it via subsidiary treaties with the local rulers. The Shekhawat Rajputs were still in nominal control, but their real power began to fade as the British took control of the region.

Mandawa, a jewel in the Shekhawati region of Rajasthan, has long been celebrated for its grandeur, historical significance, and cultural vibrancy. Known for its stunning havelis adorned with intricate frescoes, bustling trade routes, and thriving economy, Mandawa was a vital hub in pre-colonial India. However, the colonial era marked a turning point in the town's history. With the advent of British rule, Mandawa experienced profound transformations, resulting in economic decline, the migration of its merchant class, and the waning influence of its Rajput rulers. By the time India gained independence, Mandawa had been relegated from a thriving economic and cultural center to a shadow of its former self, though its artistic and architectural legacy endured as a reminder of its glorious past.

Mandawa in the Pre-Colonial Era

Before delving into the colonial period, it is essential to understand the foundation upon which Mandawa's prosperity was built. Established in the 18th century by the Shekhawat Rajputs, Mandawa thrived as a trade outpost along the caravan routes that connected India to Central Asia, Persia, and the Middle East. The Shekhawat rulers provided security and patronage to merchants, creating a conducive environment for commerce.

The town became a magnet for Marwari merchants, an enterprising business community from Rajasthan. These merchants played a pivotal role in Mandawa's development, investing their wealth in the construction of grand havelis, temples, and water reservoirs. The frescoes on these havelis depicted mythological tales, everyday life, and even colonial influences, reflecting the cosmopolitan character of Mandawa during its zenith.

The Advent of British Rule

The British East India Company's expansion into Rajasthan and subsequent establishment of colonial rule in India brought sweeping changes to the country's political, economic, and social landscapes. While the Shekhawati region, including Mandawa, was not directly annexed by the British, it came under their influence through subsidiary alliances. The Shekhawat Rajputs, who governed Mandawa, retained nominal control but were subordinated to British political agents.

This indirect rule weakened the authority of the Shekhawat rulers. Their ability to invest in the town's infrastructure, promote trade, and maintain local order was significantly curtailed. British policies prioritized the consolidation of power and revenue extraction, often at the expense of local economies like that of Mandawa.

The Decline of Trade and Commerce

One of the most significant factors contributing to Mandawa's decline during the colonial era was the disruption of traditional trade networks. Mandawa had flourished as a stop along caravan routes that facilitated the movement of goods such as textiles, spices, and precious metals. However, the British introduced modern transportation infrastructure, including railways and ports, which redirected trade to major colonial urban centers like Calcutta (Kolkata), Bombay (Mumbai), and Madras (Chennai).

The construction of railways bypassed towns like Mandawa, effectively isolating them from the new trade networks. Goods that were once transported overland by caravans now moved swiftly and more efficiently by rail and sea. As a result, Mandawa's role as a trade hub diminished, and its economy began to stagnate.

Migration of the Marwari Merchants

The Marwari merchants, who had been the backbone of Mandawa's prosperity, adapted to these changes by migrating to the emerging colonial cities. The economic opportunities in urban centers, coupled with the decline of traditional caravan trade, compelled many Marwaris to relocate. In cities like Calcutta, they established themselves as prominent traders, financiers, and industrialists, playing a crucial role in India's colonial economy.

While this migration underscored the Marwaris' entrepreneurial spirit, it also left Mandawa economically and socially depleted. The grand havelis that had once symbolized their wealth and cultural patronage stood abandoned or fell into disrepair. The vibrant bazaars and bustling trade fairs that had defined Mandawa's character became less frequent, signaling the town's waning significance.

Cultural and Artistic Impact

Mandawa's artistic heritage, particularly its frescoed havelis, suffered during this period of decline. These havelis had been commissioned by wealthy merchants as expressions of their affluence and artistic sensibilities. The frescoes depicted a unique blend of traditional themes and colonial influences, ranging from Hindu mythology to European architecture and industrial advancements like railways and telegraphs.

However, with the migration of their owners and the economic downturn, the maintenance of these havelis was neglected. The harsh desert climate, combined with a lack of resources for preservation, led to the gradual deterioration of these architectural marvels. While the frescoes remained a testament to Mandawa's rich cultural history, their fading vibrancy mirrored the town's diminishing fortunes.

The Decline of the Shekhawat Rulers

The Shekhawat rulers of Mandawa, once powerful custodians of the region, saw their authority erode under British colonial rule. The British strategy of indirect governance through princely states effectively reduced the Shekhawat chiefs to mere figureheads. They retained ceremonial roles but were stripped of significant administrative and fiscal powers.

This decline in political influence also affected their ability to act as patrons of art, culture, and infrastructure. The fort of Mandawa, which had been a symbol of Rajput power, became less of a strategic stronghold and more of a relic of a bygone era. The rulers' diminished capacity to support local development further accelerated Mandawa's decline.

Socio-Economic Changes in the Region

The colonial focus on industrialization and revenue generation had far-reaching socio-economic implications for Mandawa and the broader Shekhawati region. The agrarian population, already struggling with the arid climate and limited resources, found it increasingly difficult to sustain themselves. The lack of investment in local industries and infrastructure under British rule compounded these challenges.

Additionally, the migration of the merchant class created a social vacuum in Mandawa. The absence of their wealth and influence affected not only the town's economy but also its cultural and social life. Festivals, trade fairs, and artistic patronage became less frequent, leading to a sense of stagnation.

Mandawa's Enduring Legacy

Despite its decline during the colonial era, Mandawa retained elements of its historical and cultural identity. Its fort and havelis continued to attract attention, albeit as relics of a once-thriving town. The frescoes, though faded, remained a source of fascination for those who visited Mandawa, offering glimpses into the town's artistic and historical richness.

In the post-colonial period, Mandawa began to reinvent itself as a heritage destination. Efforts to preserve its architectural and cultural treasures gained momentum, driven by a growing recognition of their value. Tourism emerged as a new economic lifeline, bringing visitors from around the world to explore Mandawa's unique heritage.

The colonial era was a period of profound transformation for Mandawa, marking the decline of its economic, political, and cultural prominence. The disruption of traditional trade networks, migration of the merchant class, and weakening of the Shekhawat rulers contributed to the town's diminished status. Yet, Mandawa's legacy endures in its artistic and architectural heritage, which stands as a testament to its glorious past.

Today, Mandawa serves as a poignant reminder of the complex interplay between local history and global forces. Its story highlights the challenges faced by traditional economies in adapting to modernity and underscores the importance of preserving cultural heritage in the face of change. While the colonial era may have marked the decline of Mandawa, it also laid the groundwork for its reinvention as a cultural and historical treasure, ensuring that its legacy continues to inspire and captivate future generations.

3.MODERN MANDAWA

3.1 Modern Mandawa: A Reflection of Tradition and Transformation

A town rich in art, culture, and history, Mandawa is situated in Rajasthan, India's dry Shekhawati area. Mandawa reflects the dynamic forces that have influenced India's past and present, from its beginnings as a flourishing commercial hub throughout the pre-colonial and colonial periods to its transition in the modern day. Mandawa is currently at a crossroads where tradition and modernity collide, juggling the needs of modern living with the preservation of its legacy. This story examines Mandawa's socioeconomic changes, difficulties it endures, and its significance in Rajasthan's cultural landscape as it progresses into the modern day. Tourists have long been drawn to Mandawa because of its historical significance and stunning architecture, but in recent decades, the town has experienced substantial change, becoming "Modern Mandawa." A contemporary town has replaced a traditional village for a number of reasons, such as increased tourism, better infrastructure, and an emphasis on cultural preservation. A combination of Rajput, Mughal, and Marwari aesthetics shaped Mandawa's distinctive architectural style, which gained recognition throughout time. Exquisite havelis, or traditional houses, were constructed by Mandawa's affluent merchants and decorated with exquisite murals that portrayed religious themes, images from royal life, and local folktales. Due in large part to these frescoes, Mandawa has earned the nickname "open-air art gallery." The most recognizable architectural element of Mandawa is the havelis, which serve as reminders of the wealth and influence of the merchant families who formerly resided in the town. The Chokhani Double Haveli, Gulab Rai Ladia Haveli, and Murmuria Haveli are a few of the most well-known havelis.

3.2 Geography and Demographics: The Changing Landscape

Mandawa is located in the heart of the Shekhawati region in Rajasthan, an area historically known for its arid conditions, vibrant culture, and picturesque havelis adorned with intricate frescoes. The town lies about 190 kilometers north of Jaipur, the state capital, and has a population of approximately 30,000 to 35,000 people. While the town is predominantly rural, the surrounding region has become increasingly urbanized in recent decades, attracting both tourists and investors. The demographics of Mandawa reflect a mixture of agricultural workers, artisans, traders, and families involved in small-scale industry. Over the years, a significant portion of the local population has shifted from traditional agricultural occupations to small-scale businesses and tourism-related activities.

Geographically, Mandawa is part of the desert region, characterized by sandy terrain and limited rainfall, which has shaped its socio-economic fabric. However, the introduction of irrigation systems, including water harvesting techniques and wells, has enabled the growth of agriculture in certain parts of the town. Wheat, barley, and pulses are among the major crops grown in the region, although agriculture remains supplementary to other forms of livelihood. The establishment of better road connectivity to urban centers such as Jaipur and Delhi has provided greater access to markets, further integrating Mandawa into the broader economic framework of Rajasthan.

3.3 Economic Transformation: From Agriculture to Tourism and Commerce

Tourism has played a critical role in the transformation of Mandawa. In recent years, the town has seen an influx of domestic and international tourists who visit for its heritage, art, and cultural experience. The state government of Rajasthan, along with local authorities, has recognized the potential of Mandawa as a tourist destination and has invested in its development.

The rise in tourism has led to the establishment of a variety of hotels, resorts, and guesthouses that offer modern amenities while still maintaining a traditional Rajasthani architectural style. These establishments are often housed in old havelis and mansions, creating a unique experience for visitors who want to experience the royal lifestyle of Mandawa's merchant families while enjoying contemporary comforts.

The economy of Mandawa has undergone significant transformation in recent decades. In the modern era, tourism has become a central pillar of the town's economy. The heritage of Mandawa—its havelis, frescoes, and forts—attracts both domestic and international tourists. These structures, once symbols of the town's prosperity in the colonial period, are now the town's biggest assets, offering a glimpse into Rajasthan's aristocratic past.

As Rajasthan, and India as a whole, became more accessible to tourists, Mandawa's havelis gained recognition for their unique architectural style. The frescoes that adorn the walls of these mansions—depicting scenes of royal life, mythology, and early Western influence—attracted art enthusiasts, historians, and curious travelers. In response, local entrepreneurs have developed a range of tourism-related businesses, including hotels, guided tours, and cultural performances. Many of the town's traditional havelis have been converted into boutique hotels or guesthouses, offering travelers the chance to experience the grandeur of Rajasthan's architectural heritage. These hotels, while preserving the traditional aesthetics, offer modern amenities, thus catering to the needs of a more contemporary traveler.

Alongside tourism, Mandawa has also seen growth in small-scale commerce. The traditional bazaars, which were once vibrant centers of trade in textiles, spices, and opium during the colonial period, have evolved into bustling marketplaces that cater to both locals and visitors. The town's handicrafts, particularly textiles, pottery, and leather goods, are popular among tourists seeking authentic Rajasthani souvenirs. Small industries, including textile manufacturing and carpentry, contribute to the local economy, providing employment to a significant portion of the population. The export of local handicrafts has enabled Mandawa to participate in global markets, connecting it to international trade networks.

3.4 Handicrafts and Local Industries

Mandawa is known for its beautiful handicrafts, particularly in textiles, leather, and pottery. Local artisans continue to produce hand-painted textiles, intricate jewelry, and handcrafted pottery, which are sold in markets around the town and at local shops. These items are popular among tourists who seek authentic Rajasthani souvenirs, and the craft industry has provided a livelihood for many of Mandawa's residents.

Additionally, the town's local industries have adapted to cater to modern tastes. Many of the traditional handicrafts are now marketed online and are sold to global buyers. This has helped increase the visibility of Mandawa's art and crafts on the international stage.

Despite this growth in tourism and commerce, Mandawa still grapples with challenges related to rural poverty and unemployment. Although there has been a shift in the workforce, agriculture remains an important source of livelihood for many families. The reliance on traditional farming practices and limited access to modern technologies poses challenges for the town's long-term economic development. Furthermore, the growth of the tourism industry has created a dependence on seasonal influxes of visitors, which can be unpredictable. Nevertheless, Mandawa's increasing connectivity to major cities, improved infrastructure, and the growing interest in heritage tourism have positioned the town as an emerging center of economic activity in the Shekhawati region.

3.5 The Role of Local Government and Private Stakeholders

The local government and private stakeholders have been key players in the modernization of Mandawa. The government's efforts to promote tourism through initiatives such as the Rajasthan Heritage Development and Promotion Board have been instrumental in increasing the visibility of Mandawa on the global tourism map. Moreover, private investors and businesses have also contributed to the town's development, especially in the hospitality sector, by restoring old havelis and converting them into boutique hotels, art galleries, and museums.

The restoration of these heritage properties has helped preserve the town's cultural legacy while giving it a modern twist. Many of these restored buildings now serve dual purposes: they are both working businesses and historical landmarks, attracting visitors interested in the town's rich past as well as its future.

3.6 Cultural Preservation and Challenges of Modernization

One of the most striking features of Modern Mandawa is the seamless blend of old and new. While the town has adapted to modern needs and desires, it has not sacrificed its traditional character. The architectural style of Mandawa remains true to its roots, with the town still being home to stunning havelis adorned with frescoes, jharokhas (overhanging windows), and ornate courtyards.

The integration of modern elements has been subtle yet effective. The new constructions in Mandawa, including hotels, restaurants, and other public buildings, often take inspiration from traditional Rajasthani architecture. They feature elements like arches, decorative woodwork, and the use of local stone, blending the old with the new. This has allowed the town to maintain its cultural essence while catering to contemporary needs. Mandawa is not only a town of economic significance but also a cultural hub. The preservation of its architectural and artistic heritage remains a priority for both local authorities and the community. The town's havelis, which feature intricate frescoes with scenes ranging from mythological figures to depictions of Western technology, remain key attractions. However, as Mandawa transitions into the modern era, the challenge of preserving its cultural heritage while adapting to modern needs has become increasingly complex.

In the early 2000s, Mandawa was recognized as a heritage town, and efforts to protect its architectural legacy have gained momentum in recent years. Many of the town's havelis, which had fallen into disrepair, have been restored with the help of local and national preservation initiatives. International organizations, such as UNESCO, have also supported efforts to conserve the town's frescoes and historical structures. The implementation of tourism-oriented conservation strategies has ensured that the town's historic charm is maintained while simultaneously catering to the needs of modern tourism.

However, the preservation of Mandawa's cultural heritage is not without its challenges. The influx of tourism has put pressure on the town's infrastructure and the local population. The need for modern amenities, such as roads, electricity, and sewage systems, conflicts with the preservation of traditional architecture and design. The installation of modern conveniences within heritage structures, while necessary, poses risks to the authenticity and integrity of the town's historic sites.

The town's cultural fabric also faces challenges from the forces of modernization. As younger generations of Mandawa's population increasingly seek education and employment opportunities in larger cities, traditional crafts and practices risk becoming obsolete. The younger population, with limited interest in continuing ancestral business ventures, may contribute to the erosion of local culture and skills. The artisans who once hand-painted the intricate frescoes or crafted traditional textiles are now fewer in number, and their craft is not always passed down to the next generation. However, various cultural programs and workshops organized by local authorities and NGOs have been instrumental in educating the youth about the value of their heritage, ensuring the continuity of these artistic traditions.

3.7 Education and Infrastructure Development

With tourism driving the local economy, Mandawa has seen substantial improvements in its infrastructure. Roads have been upgraded, and new transportation links have been established to make the town more accessible from major cities like Jaipur, Delhi, and Agra. The introduction of new modes of transport, such as taxis and buses, has made travel to Mandawa more convenient, especially for tourists who seek a cultural getaway.

Additionally, modern amenities like internet access, mobile connectivity, and clean water supply have been introduced, making life easier for both locals and tourists. The presence of medical facilities, improved sanitation, and a burgeoning local market have all contributed to the growing livability and attractiveness of the town.

Mandawa has seen steady progress in education and infrastructure in the modern era, although the pace of change has been slower than in urban centers. The literacy rate in Mandawa has improved significantly, with local schools offering education up to the secondary level. Many young residents now pursue higher education in nearby cities like Jaipur and Delhi, contributing to the region's growing middle class. Furthermore, vocational training in areas such as hospitality management, arts, and crafts has been encouraged to support the growing tourism industry.

Infrastructure development, however, remains a work in progress. While Mandawa has benefited from improved road connectivity through the Rajasthan State Highway network, the town still struggles with issues such as unreliable electricity, poor waste management, and inadequate healthcare facilities. The tourism boom has brought some improvements in infrastructure, such as the development of new hotels, roads, and public spaces. However, the local government faces significant challenges in balancing the needs of the population with the demands of a growing tourist economy.

The internet and mobile connectivity have been a recent boon for Mandawa. These technological advancements have enabled locals to access global markets, promote their businesses online, and learn about new developments in various fields. The younger generation, in particular, has embraced these tools to stay connected with the wider world and explore opportunities beyond the confines of their traditional occupations.

3.8 Social Changes and Challenges

Mandawa has undergone several social changes in the modern era, particularly with regard to gender, caste, and class. Historically, Mandawa, like much of rural India, was a patriarchal society where women had limited access to education and economic opportunities. However, the influence of modern education and changing social norms has led to a gradual shift in gender roles. More women in Mandawa are now pursuing education, working in local businesses, and even taking leadership roles in community organizations. Although challenges remain, including traditional expectations and limited opportunities for women in rural areas, the growing participation of women in the workforce is a sign of positive change.

Caste dynamics in Mandawa have also evolved, although social stratification continues to be a significant aspect of life in the town. Mandawa's population is diverse, with communities from different castes, including the Marwari business class, Brahmins, Rajputs, and artisans, living and working together. While caste-based discrimination remains a concern in rural areas, the modern influences of education, urbanization, and the national push for equality have begun to reduce these divisions, at least in the more visible aspects of public life.

Class differences in Mandawa are also more pronounced today. While tourism and small-scale industries have generated wealth for certain families, the majority of the population still lives in poverty, relying on agriculture and seasonal labor. Many residents of Mandawa, particularly those working in the traditional crafts or low-wage industries, face socio-economic challenges that impede upward mobility. This economic divide is one of the key issues that the town must address as it moves forward into the future.

3.9 Mandawa's Future: Prospects and Sustainability

Mandawa, a town renowned for its rich cultural heritage and vibrant architectural legacy, has witnessed significant growth in recent years, driven largely by tourism. As the town moves toward the future, its prospects look promising, but ensuring sustainability will be key to maintaining its unique character while supporting modern development. This balancing act will involve careful consideration of environmental, economic, and cultural factors to ensure Mandawa's long-term success.

Economic Prospects: Tourism and Heritage Conservation

Mandawa's tourism industry is central to its economic growth. The town's well-preserved havelis, frescoes, and historical charm make it a sought-after destination, particularly for those interested in Rajasthan's culture and heritage. As tourism continues to thrive, the potential for increased revenue and job creation grows. This can lead to improved local infrastructure, better educational opportunities, and enhanced services for residents.

However, the challenge lies in ensuring that tourism does not overshadow the town's heritage. To secure long-term economic prosperity, Mandawa must embrace sustainable tourism practices. This means focusing on responsible tourism that preserves the local culture while offering a high-quality experience for visitors. Encouraging eco-friendly hotels, promoting cultural heritage walks, and limiting overdevelopment will be critical to sustaining both the town's economy and its traditional charm. Preserving Mandawa's heritage has been a key priority for both the local community and the government. Many of the town's frescoes have been carefully restored, and efforts have been made to protect these intricate artworks from the ravages of time and weather. The frescoes themselves remain a central aspect of Mandawa's cultural identity, attracting art lovers and history enthusiasts. The economy of Mandawa has traditionally been based on agriculture, trade, and the wealth accumulated by merchant families. However, in recent years, the local economy has shifted towards tourism, hospitality, and handicrafts. The demand for Rajasthani textiles, pottery, and metal crafts has led to a resurgence of traditional crafts in the town, providing local artisans with a steady income.`

`

A major part of this preservation effort is the Mandawa Heritage Walk, which allows visitors to explore the town's most significant havelis, temples, and landmarks. Through this initiative, visitors can learn about the town's history, architecture, and culture while also supporting the local economy by purchasing handicrafts and goods from the town's artisans.

Cultural Sustainability: Preserving the Heritage

Mandawa's frescoes, havelis, and historic buildings are integral to its identity. As tourism increases, preserving these cultural assets becomes crucial. The town has made efforts to restore and protect its historic structures, but this requires continuous investment and vigilance. The Mandawa Heritage Walk, which guides visitors through the town's significant landmarks, is an example of how cultural assets can be showcased responsibly. While Mandawa is often celebrated for its historical frescoes, the town is also home to a growing modern art scene. Many local artists have taken inspiration from traditional Rajasthani art forms and infused them with contemporary techniques and styles. The town hosts art exhibitions and workshops that showcase the work of both local and international artists.

In addition to visual arts, Mandawa has a rich tradition of folk music and dance, which is an important part of the town's cultural identity. The introduction of modern music and dance forms, including performances of Bollywood hits and fusion genres, has created a dynamic cultural landscape that caters to a wide range of tastes.

For the future, local authorities and communities must collaborate to develop strategies that protect these architectural treasures. This could include implementing strict regulations for building alterations, supporting the restoration of traditional art forms, and educating visitors about the importance of cultural preservation. Creating a balance between heritage conservation and modern living will be essential for Mandawa's sustainable growth.

Environmental Sustainability: Balancing Development and Conservation

Mandawa's location in the arid region of Rajasthan presents challenges related to water management and environmental conservation. As the town grows, its infrastructure and resources must be managed sustainably to avoid strain on natural resources. The introduction of water conservation technologies, such as rainwater harvesting and efficient irrigation practices, can help mitigate water scarcity issues.

Additionally, the expansion of Mandawa should be planned to minimize environmental degradation. Green building initiatives, waste management systems, and energy-efficient technologies should be encouraged. These measures will not only improve the quality of life for residents but also contribute to Mandawa's reputation as an environmentally responsible destination.

Social and Community Development: Inclusivity and Livelihoods

The future of Mandawa also depends on fostering an inclusive, thriving community. Ensuring access to healthcare, education, and economic opportunities for all residents will be crucial as the town grows. Promoting local crafts, supporting small businesses, and providing skill development programs will help create sustainable livelihoods for the people of Mandawa.

Furthermore, engaging the local population in decisions about development and conservation will ensure that growth aligns with the needs of the community. As the town continues to modernize, involving residents in the planning process will be essential to avoid displacement and ensure that Mandawa's growth benefits everyone.

3.10 Conclusion: A Balanced Future

Mandawa's future holds tremendous potential, with its blend of rich heritage, vibrant tourism, and growing economy. However, its sustainability will depend on the careful balancing of economic growth, cultural preservation, environmental stewardship, and social inclusion. By adopting sustainable practices and fostering collaboration among stakeholders, Mandawa can navigate the challenges of modernization while preserving the qualities that make it a unique and enduring destination. Agriculture still plays a role in Mandawa's economy, with the region growing crops like millet, wheat, and barley. However, the agricultural sector has seen less growth compared to the tourism and handicraft industries. Modern farming techniques, including the use of drip irrigation and mechanized farming tools, have been introduced to increase crop yields and make farming more sustainable in the region's arid climate.

While Modern Mandawa has seen significant development, it faces several challenges that need to be addressed in order to ensure its continued success as a cultural and economic hub.

One of the primary concerns is the preservation of its cultural heritage amid the pressures of modernization and commercialization.

The influx of tourism has put a strain on Mandawa's delicate frescoes and heritage buildings. As the town grows, there is a risk that the authenticity of these structures could be compromised in the pursuit of modernization. It will be important for both the government and the local community to strike a balance between preserving Mandawa's cultural heritage and embracing modern developments.

The rise in tourism has brought economic benefits to Mandawa, but it has also created issues such as overcrowding, environmental degradation, and resource strain. Sustainable tourism practices will be essential for the town's future growth, ensuring that the benefits of tourism are distributed equitably while protecting the town's natural and cultural resources.

As Mandawa becomes more urbanized, there are concerns about the impact of rapid growth on the town's infrastructure, quality of life, and traditional way of life. Managing urbanization in a way that maintains the town's historical charm while catering to the needs of a modern population will be a key challenge for local authorities.

Modern Mandawa is a fascinating example of how a traditional town can evolve while retaining its cultural heritage. The fusion of the old and the new in architecture, culture, and economy has created a unique town that is both a living museum and a vibrant, modern community. With its historical significance, beautiful frescoes, thriving tourism industry, and growing local economy, Mandawa stands as a testament to the resilience of tradition in the face of modernization. Its future, however, will depend on balancing progress with preservation, ensuring that this historic town continues to flourish while retaining the qualities that make it so special.

4. HAVELIS OF MANDAWA

4.1 Havelis of Mandawa: A Testament to Rajasthan's Artistic Brilliance

In the arid lands of Rajasthan, amidst the golden sands of the Shekhawati region, lies the enchanting town of Mandawa. Renowned for its breathtaking havelis, Mandawa is a treasure trove of art, architecture, and history. These havelis, grand mansions built by wealthy merchants during the 18th and 19th centuries, are adorned with intricate frescoes and carvings that narrate stories of mythology, tradition, and a bygone era of prosperity. Often referred to as an "Open-Air Art Gallery," Mandawa's havelis stand as enduring symbols of Rajasthan's rich cultural heritage. In the Shekhawati region of Rajasthan, the quaint town of Mandawa emerges as a treasure trove of history and artistry, renowned for its magnificent havelis. These grand mansions, constructed by affluent merchants in the 18th and 19th centuries, are adorned with intricate frescoes and carvings that narrate tales of mythology, culture, and everyday life. Mandawa, often described as an "Open-Air Art Gallery," encapsulates the essence of Rajasthan's architectural and artistic heritage. The havelis are not just architectural marvels but also visual storytellers, preserving a vibrant past and showcasing the craftsmanship of a bygone era. Mandawa's rise to prominence can be traced back to its strategic location on ancient trade routes that connected India to the Middle East and beyond. As trade flourished, wealthy merchants settled in Mandawa, creating an opulent legacy through these havelis. These mansions became symbols of wealth and status, meticulously designed to reflect the grandeur and sophistication of their owners. Over time, the havelis have become a cultural landmark, attracting visitors from around the world to marvel at their artistic brilliance.

The architecture of the havelis in Mandawa reflects a harmonious blend of Rajputana and Mughal styles, characterized by their grand facades, enclosed balconies, and central courtyards. These architectural elements were not merely ornamental but served functional purposes, such as ensuring privacy and ventilation. The doors and windows of the havelis are often embellished with elaborate carvings, showcasing floral patterns, geometric designs, and depictions of mythological figures. The intricate woodwork stands as a testament to the exceptional skill of the artisans who crafted these masterpieces.

The frescoes that adorn the walls, ceilings, and doorways of the havelis are the true essence of their artistic allure. Painted with natural pigments, these vibrant artworks have remarkably stood the test of time. The frescoes depict a wide array of themes, ranging from mythological stories and religious motifs to historical events and scenes of everyday life. Stories from the Mahabharata and Ramayana, portraits of Hindu deities, and depictions of royal processions and battles are intricately painted, bringing the walls of these mansions to life. Interestingly, the frescoes also reflect the changing times, with European influences becoming evident in the 19th century. Paintings of steam engines, hot air balloons, and colonial officials illustrate the region's exposure to global influences during the colonial period. These European-inspired elements are seamlessly integrated with traditional Rajasthani themes, creating a unique fusion of styles that is both fascinating and visually captivating. Each haveli in Mandawa has its own unique character and charm, but all share a common thread of artistic excellence. The Jhunjhunwala Haveli, for instance, is known for its richly detailed frescoes that depict scenes from Hindu mythology and rural life. The Murmuria Haveli stands out for its blend of traditional and modern influences, with paintings of deities juxtaposed with images of trains and European figures. The Goenka Double Haveli, with its symmetrical design and dual wings, showcases intricate carvings and vibrant frescoes that reflect the opulence of its time. The Chokhani Haveli and Hanuman Prasad Goenka Haveli are equally remarkable, each offering a feast for the eyes with their bold colors and imaginative compositions.

Towering above the town is the Mandawa Fort, a symbol of the region's royal heritage. Built in the 18th century, the fort features grand arches, mirror work, and elaborate frescoes, complementing the artistic beauty of the havelis. Today, the fort has been converted into a heritage hotel, allowing visitors to experience the grandeur of Rajasthan's history firsthand. The panoramic views from the fort's terraces further enhance the allure of Mandawa, offering a breathtaking glimpse of the town and its surrounding landscapes. The havelis of Mandawa are more than just architectural wonders; they are cultural treasures that offer a window into the past. They encapsulate the socio-economic dynamics of an era when trade, art, and tradition flourished in harmony. The frescoes, in particular, serve as a repository of stories, capturing the beliefs, values, and aspirations of the people who created them. They also highlight the adaptability and openness of the region, as seen in the seamless integration of European motifs into traditional art forms. However, the havelis face significant challenges in the modern era. Neglect, urbanization, and exposure to the elements have led to the deterioration of many frescoes and structural elements. Efforts to preserve and restore these cultural gems are underway, with heritage organizations and local authorities working to protect Mandawa's artistic legacy. Sustainable tourism and community involvement are crucial in ensuring the longevity of these treasures, allowing future generations to appreciate their historical and cultural significance. The havelis of Mandawa are a testament to Rajasthan's artistic brilliance and enduring heritage. Their intricate frescoes, grand architecture, and rich history make them a must-visit for anyone seeking to explore the depths of India's cultural past. Walking through the streets of Mandawa is like stepping into a living museum, where every corner reveals a masterpiece and every fresco tells a story. For those who venture to this enchanting town, the havelis of Mandawa offer an unforgettable journey into a world of timeless beauty, leaving an indelible mark on the hearts of all who visit.

4.2 A Walk Through History

The history of Mandawa is deeply intertwined with the rise of the merchant class in Rajasthan. In the 18th century, Mandawa was established as a trading hub along the Silk Road, connecting the ports of Gujarat to northern India. Prosperous traders and merchants settled here, amassing great wealth through trade in silk, opium, and spices. To display their affluence and secure their legacy, these merchants built opulent havelis decorated with exquisite frescoes and carvings, transforming the town into a center of artistic excellence.

These havelis served not just as homes but also as status symbols, with their elaborate architecture and detailed artwork showcasing the owner's wealth and aesthetic sensibilities. Over the centuries, these structures became cultural landmarks, preserving the legacy of a flourishing era in Mandawa's history.

4.3 Architectural Splendor

The havelis of Mandawa are celebrated for their architectural brilliance, which combines traditional Rajputana and Mughal styles. These mansions are characterized by grand facades, intricately carved wooden doors, and jharokhas (enclosed balconies) that overlook the streets below. The central courtyards, often surrounded by multiple stories of rooms, were designed to accommodate extended families while promoting ventilation and privacy.

The craftsmanship of the wooden doors and windows is a testament to the skill of Rajasthani artisans. Delicate floral patterns, geometric designs, and mythological figures are carved with precision, turning even the smallest architectural elements into works of art. The use of natural pigments and materials ensures that these havelis retain their vibrant appearance even after centuries of weathering.

As a result, this expansive, artistically rich environment evokes the scent of hundreds of well painted temples, havelis, and cenotaphs that have painted their histories and traditions in the widest murals over millennia. A large number of Marwari merchants who accumulated wealth via trading gave these architectural gems to the globe. The havelis of Mandawa and the Shekhawati area are pulsing canvases of art and culture, rich in the heritage of the past.

The origins of Shekhawati's traditional mansions, or havelis, can be traced to the merchant-businessmen from the Vaishya and Agrawal groups who made their fortunes trading in textiles, spices, and opium. This wealth was not limited to the vaults or tangible accomplishments. It was architectural splendor, and each haveli became a residence and a testament to your prosperity. Although the grandeur of these towering facades contributes to their appeal, the actual splendor of those havelis conveys a completely different message. To preserve Shekhawati fresco art, it is located on the walls where rich tradition meets the modern world. This spans more than 100 kilometers, and the area is covered in hundreds of buildings that are colorful and vibrantly painted murals. In addition to depicting scenes from the Ramayana and Mahabharata, they also paint images of festivals like Holi and Gangaur, as well as mythology and folklore and everyday objects like the Indian gods Krishna and Shiva and Lakshmi. The paintings' method is astounding; the artists employed natural pigments like kesar and kajal, which have endured throughout time and produce incredibly vivid colors.

4.4 Mandawa: The Pride of Shekhawati

On a visit to Mandawa, one finds a one-time market town jewel, strung with havelis echoing a bygone era of where wealth converged with art. Two of the grandest examples are the Gulab Rai Ladia Haveli and Murmuria Haveli, whose frescoes sport colours speaking of myth, history, and even modernity. Over there stands sprawling Mandawa Fort, which used to be a critical trading post but is now a hotel—a living reminder of what the town used to be, prosperous.

Time does not change in the walled city of Mandawa. Wandering through narrow Bustling streets and frescoes transport you to the world of 19th century India, curiously interwoven with symbols of European Motor cars, Gramophones, and even British officers. Witness a demonstration of cultural exchange that silently shaped this region. But time changes nothing in frescoes: vivid and their stories so true.

4.5 Nawalgarh-A riot of Colours

While Mandawa could be the heart of Shekhawati, Nawalgarh is its pulse. This busy town has a sprawling marketplace surrounded by well-planned architecture. Going through the kaleidoscope of painted havelis is a huge sensory overload in this very town. A few examples are Murarka Haveli, Roop Niwas Kothi, and Dr. Ramnath Poddar Haveli with frescoes that range from religious depictions to intricate geometric designs.

This haveli itself is a museum that belongs to Dr. Ramnath Poddar, having more than 750 frescoes on its walls displaying the beauty of Rajasthan in its art and culture. Roop Niwas Kothi, as one may say, is affectionately also called the Horse Lovers' Paradise-abandoning one back in time when royalty and elegance ruled the day. It is too easy to get lost in the stories these walls will tell you with such an imposing structure and beautifully restored murals.

The Art of Shekhawati

Art lies at the nucleus of Shekhawati's charm-a uniqueness interfacing Rajput with Mughal. The havelis were a sort of visual diary detailing life, belief, and aspiration regarding the merchant families who built them. Frescoes of early times were dominated by geometric designs and floral motifs; later works were much more expressive, dealing with tales from mythology coupled with chronicling life in the Rajput courts. Repetitive sequences of the themes of folk mythology and Krishna Lila started to appear in the Ragmala paintings, but with time, these walls started narrating new stories. The British invasion left their marks on them, and images of motorcars and aeroplanes and even women from Europe carrying gramophones started to appear. Fresh coats in Shekhawati frescoes started looking like a mirror to the world beyond. Indeed, striking details capture both tradition and change in storytelling.

Preserve a legacy

The government, along with other such organisations, have been working to save what was, indeed, a considerable art heritage of Shekhawati during these years. The Jawahar Kala Kendra at Jaipur and the National Crafts Museum at Delhi house Shekhawati paintings for a wider section of the audience. But steps taken thus far are not enough to save these fragile works of art, whose fate still appears to hang in the balance. You feel that you're not just witnessing history through walking on the streets of Shekhawati but are being part of it. More than buildings, the fading frescoes in the facade of these havelis enclose stories that are awaiting narration, rest etched in stone.

4.6 The Enchantment of Traditional Havelis

From the Aath Haveli complex in Nawalgarh to the Sone Chandi ki Haveli in Jhunjhunu, these havelis do form a bequest of art on their own in Shekhawati. Almost every small town of Shekhawati narrates a new story and provides a new perspective and way to experience the art of this region. Be it the royal Alsisar Mahal now housing the celebrity-studded Magnetic Fields Festival, or the serene beauty of Ramgarh Fresco Hotel, Shekhawati promises to be a feast for all senses for every art connoisseur.

More than history, such painted havelis are the soul of Rajasthan: a place where art and culture are made to sell and buy the miracles that are in front of us. It is in the delicacy of the strokes of the brush, in the saturation of colours, that heritage lives in these murals; it shines as a gleam, reminding of what has been brought into this world, as it forward would seem to roll perpetually. Almost as if in Shekhawati, art was not viewed but lived and breathed in. The pale frescoes and beautiful structures of the havelis open you up to a world where stories are painted on walls, and where history as much belongs to the present as it does to the past. So, in case one finds themselves in Rajasthan, well, there is that detour toward the havelis of Mandawa. You will leave, not with memories, but with stories etched into your soul.

4.7 The Frescoes: Stories on Walls

What sets the havelis of Mandawa apart are their frescoes, which cover walls, ceilings, and even doorways. These frescoes are more than mere decorations; they are visual narratives that capture the essence of Rajasthani culture, religion, and history. Created using natural dyes and pigments, these paintings are remarkably well-preserved and vibrant even today.

The themes of these frescoes are diverse and include:

- **Mythological Tales**: Scenes from the Ramayana, Mahabharata, and the lives of Hindu deities such as Krishna and Shiva dominate the frescoes. These stories, painted with intricate detail, bring the divine narratives to life.

- **Historical Events**: Many frescoes depict events from Rajasthan's history, including battles, royal processions, and the exploits of Rajput kings. These paintings serve as a visual chronicle of the region's valor and grandeur.

- **Colonial Influence**: During the 19th century, European elements began to appear in the frescoes. Paintings of steam engines, gramophones, hot air balloons, and colonial figures reflect the changing times and the global connections of Mandawa's merchants.

- **Everyday Life**: Scenes of rural life, markets, and festivals provide a glimpse into the daily lives of the people of Mandawa. These frescoes capture the vibrancy and dynamism of Rajasthani culture.

Each fresco is a masterpiece, showcasing the creativity and skill of the artists who brought these stories to life. The use of bold colors, intricate patterns, and imaginative compositions makes these paintings a visual delight.

4.8 Notable Havelis of Mandawa
Jhunjhunwala Haveli

The Jhunjhunwala Haveli is one of Mandawa's most famous landmarks. Known for its elaborate frescoes, this haveli features vivid paintings of mythological figures, floral patterns, and scenes from daily life. The artistry and attention to detail in its design make it a must-visit for art enthusiasts.

Goenka Double Haveli

The Goenka Double Haveli stands out for its symmetrical design and dual wings, each adorned with exquisite frescoes and carvings. This haveli showcases the opulence and architectural ingenuity of its time.

Murmuria Haveli

A blend of tradition and modernity, the Murmuria Haveli features frescoes that incorporate both Rajasthani themes and European influences. Paintings of trains, cars, and colonial officials sit alongside depictions of deities and rural scenes, creating a fascinating fusion of styles.

Chokhani Haveli

The Chokhani Haveli is celebrated for its vibrant frescoes and intricate carvings. Its walls and ceilings are adorned with paintings that depict Hindu mythology, royal processions, and festive celebrations. The bold colors and imaginative compositions make it a visual feast.

Hanuman Prasad Goenka Haveli

Dedicated to religious and spiritual themes, the Hanuman Prasad Goenka Haveli features detailed paintings of Hindu gods and goddesses. These frescoes exude a sense of devotion and artistry, making this haveli a spiritually enriching experience for visitors.

The Mandawa Fort

Overlooking the town is the majestic Mandawa Fort, a symbol of the region's royal heritage. Built in the 18th century by Thakur Nawal Singh, the fort features grand arches, elaborate frescoes, and intricate mirror work. Today, it has been converted into a heritage hotel, allowing visitors to experience the grandeur of Rajasthan's royal past. From its terraces, one can enjoy panoramic views of Mandawa and its surrounding landscapes.

The Mandawa Fort, with its robust architecture and artistic interiors, complements the beauty of the town's havelis and adds to its charm.

Cultural Significance

Mandawa's havelis are more than architectural marvels; they are cultural landmarks that preserve the legacy of a rich and vibrant era. These structures reflect the interplay of art, commerce, and tradition, offering insights into the lives of the merchant class and the socio-economic dynamics of the time.

The frescoes, in particular, serve as a repository of cultural narratives, encapsulating the beliefs, values, and aspirations of the people who created them. They also highlight the region's openness to new ideas and influences, as seen in the incorporation of European elements into traditional art forms.

Preservation Challenges

Despite their historical and artistic significance, the havelis of Mandawa face numerous challenges. Neglect, weathering, and urbanization have taken a toll on these structures, leading to the deterioration of their frescoes and architectural elements. Efforts are being made by government bodies, heritage conservation organizations, and private entities to restore and preserve these treasures.

Sustainable tourism practices and community involvement are crucial to ensuring the longevity of Mandawa's havelis. By raising awareness and promoting responsible tourism, it is possible to safeguard these cultural gems for future generations.

4.9 Conclusion

The havelis of Mandawa are a testament to Rajasthan's artistic brilliance and cultural heritage. With their intricate frescoes, grand architecture, and rich history, these structures offer a glimpse into a bygone era of opulence and creativity. Visiting Mandawa is like stepping into a living museum, where every corner tells a story and every fresco is a work of art.

For travelers seeking to explore the heart of Rajasthan's cultural and artistic legacy, Mandawa's havelis provide an unforgettable experience, leaving an indelible impression of the region's timeless charm.

5.DESIGN AND STRUCTURE OF THE HAVELIS

The **havelis of Mandawa** are one of the most defining features of the town's rich architectural heritage. Built primarily by wealthy merchants, these opulent mansions were designed not only as family homes but also as symbols of their prosperity, cultural sophistication, ansocial standing. The architecture of these havelis reflects a blend of traditional Rajasthani style with external influences, showcasing intricate craftsmanship and an artistic legacy that has endured for centuries.Let's explore the design, structure, layout, and key architectural elements like arches and balconies in greater detail:

5.1 Structure and Layout

The havelis of Mandawa, like other parts of Shekhawati, were built between the **18th and early 20th centuries** during a time when trade flourished. The merchants, particularly the Marwaris, accumulated wealth through commerce along the trade routes connecting Rajasthan to Central Asia, the Middle East, and beyond. This newfound affluence led them to build lavish homes that reflected both their wealth and their status within the community. The havelis were traditionally designed as large, multi-storied residences, with a layout that ensured privacy, comfort, and security while also catering to the harsh desert climate. A typical haveli consists of a central courtyard, which forms the heart of the residence. This courtyard, called the *chowk*, is surrounded by rooms, galleries, and corridors on all sides. The architecture followed a clear spatial hierarchy, separating private, semi-private, and public spaces.

The havelis often feature two or more courtyards, with one designated for the men (*mardana*) and the other for women (*zenana*). This division respected cultural norms, providing the women of the household with privacy while allowing men to entertain guests in separate areas. The rooms around the courtyards are adorned with carved wooden doors, ornate pillars, and intricately painted walls, creating a seamless blend of functionality and artistry.

Massive Scale and Grandeur: The havelis were often multi-storied and sprawling in design. They featured large, imposing facades, with intricate detailing and decorative elements on every available surface. The grand scale of these homes emphasized the affluence of the owners, with entire walls and exteriors often covered in exquisite frescoes depicting religious themes, mythological stories, historical events, and everyday life.

- **Material and Construction**: The primary building materials used in the construction of the havelis included locally available **stone, brick, and lime plaster**. The architecture also incorporated wood, particularly for the finely carved doors and windows. The plasterwork on the walls, combined with intricate fresco painting, was a hallmark of Shekhawati havelis.

- **Fortified Look**: Many of the havelis had an external appearance reminiscent of small forts or palaces. Thick walls and strong gates provided security and privacy, making them somewhat self-contained worlds for the wealthy families that resided in them.

Layout of the Havelis:

One of the most remarkable aspects of these havelis is their **architectural layout**, which followed a traditional style suited to both the climate of Rajasthan and the social customs of the time.

- **Courtyard-Centric Design**: The typical layout of a haveli was organized around a **central courtyard** (or multiple courtyards in larger havelis), which acted as the heart of the home. The courtyard was not only an architectural feature but a social space where families gathered, celebrated festivals, and conducted everyday activities.

  - **Climate Adaptation**: Given the hot and arid climate of Rajasthan, the courtyard-centric layout provided natural ventilation, ensuring that air circulated freely through the house, keeping the rooms cooler in the scorching summer heat.

  - **Privacy**: The inner courtyard also offered privacy to the family, especially the women, who could observe activities or interact with visitors from the upper floors without being seen, adhering to the **purdah system** prevalent in that era.

- **Rooms Surrounding the Courtyard**: The rooms were arranged around the courtyard in a rectangular or U-shaped pattern. These rooms had multiple functions, serving as living areas, bedrooms, storage spaces, and sometimes even trading offices or spaces for storing goods. The family members' quarters were generally on the upper floors, while the ground floor was used for business dealings, entertaining guests, and storing goods.

- o The separation of spaces ensured that while the family could live comfortably, the mercantile activities that brought wealth to the household were efficiently managed from the same building.

- **Chowks and Baithaks**: Many larger havelis had more than one **chowk** (courtyard), each serving different purposes. There might be one for the men of the family to meet business associates (the **baithak**) and another for more private family gatherings.

Arches and Balconies (Jharokhas):

The architectural beauty of the havelis is further elevated by their **ornate arches** and **balconies**, which are not only functional but also highly decorative.

- ***Multi-Tiered Balconies (Jharokhas)**: One of the most stunning features of Mandawa's havelis is the use of **jharokhas**, or overhanging balconies, which are a hallmark of **Rajput architecture**. These balconies, often protruding from the upper floors, offered views of the street below and allowed for air circulation into the rooms behind them.

  - o **Carved Stone and Woodwork**: These balconies were often made of finely carved sandstone or wood, with intricate designs that included floral patterns, geometric shapes, and sometimes figures of gods, animals, or mythical creatures.

  - o **Role in Ventilation and Privacy**: Jharokhas also served practical purposes. They provided a shaded area where women could observe the outside world while maintaining the strict privacy required by social customs. Additionally, these balconies helped cool the rooms by allowing breezes to pass through them.

Elaborate Arches: The arches in Mandawa's havelis are some of the most iconic features of the architecture. These arches are used in doorways, windows, courtyards, and balconies.

- o **Types of Arches**: The most common type is the **cusped arch**, often seen in Mughal and Rajput architecture. These arches are highly decorative and are characterized by multiple curves that form a distinct and beautiful outline.

- o **Gateway Arches (Torans)**: The gateways of the havelis often feature large arches (torans) with elaborately carved stone or wood, acting as grand entrances that set the tone for the opulence inside. Many of these arches also incorporate frescoes, further enhancing their visual appeal.

- o **Symbolism**: The arches are not only aesthetic but also symbolic, representing the wealth and status of the family and often featuring elements of religious and cultural symbolism.

5.2 Frescoes and Decorative Elements of Havelis in Mandawa

The most striking feature of Mandawa's havelis is their breathtaking frescoes that adorn both the interior and exterior walls. These frescoes were painted using natural colors derived from minerals, plants, and stones, ensuring their longevity. The themes of the frescoes range from mythological stories, religious imagery, and daily life scenes to depictions of British colonization, modern inventions like trains and gramophones, and even European influences.

The exterior facades of the havelis are richly decorated with vibrant frescoes, reflecting the wealth and taste of their owners. The motifs are often framed by elaborate arches, jharokhas (overhanging balconies), and latticed screens (*jali work*), which also enhance ventilation and light within the structure. Carved wooden doors and windows, often featuring floral and geometric patterns, further add to the charm of these buildings. The frescoes and decorative elements of the havelis in Mandawa are among the most stunning examples of artistic expression in Rajasthan. These havelis, built during the 18th to early 20th centuries, served not only as residences but also as canvases for artisans to showcase their skill and creativity. The frescoes reflect a unique blend of Indian cultural traditions, religious themes, and colonial influences, making them invaluable treasures of heritage art. The frescoes are the defining feature of Mandawa's havelis, covering both interior and exterior walls with vibrant, detailed paintings. These frescoes were created using natural pigments derived from minerals, plants, and stones, ensuring their longevity and brilliance. The walls are adorned with themes that range from:

- **Mythological and Religious Depictions**: Scenes from Hindu epics like the *Ramayana* and *Mahabharata*, as well as depictions of gods like Krishna, Shiva, and Ganesha, dominate many frescoes. These paintings often narrate stories of divine love, valor, and devotion.

- **Daily Life and Cultural Scenes**: Artisans captured the essence of everyday life, portraying activities such as processions, festivals, and markets. These images provide insights into the social and cultural practices of the time.

- **Colonial and European Influences**: Reflecting changing times, many frescoes depict European officers, British-style clothing, trains, clocks, and gramophones. These elements highlight the fusion of local tradition with colonial modernity.

The frescoes are not only colorful but also intricate, showcasing the precision and attention to detail of the artists. The themes are framed with ornate floral borders, geometric designs, and scrollwork, adding depth and dimension to the paintings.

5.3 Carved Decorative Elements:

In addition to the frescoes, the havelis feature various carved and ornamental details that enhance their aesthetic appeal:

- **Jharokhas (Overhanging Balconies)**: Beautifully carved jharokhas made of sandstone or wood are a prominent feature of Mandawa havelis. These balconies often include lattice screens (*jali work*) that provide ventilation and privacy while adding to the visual splendor of the facade.

- **Wooden Doors and Windows**: The doors and windows are meticulously carved with floral patterns, mythological motifs, and geometric designs. These carvings reflect the wealth and artistic sensibility of the haveli owners.

- **Arches and Pillars**: The arches and pillars of the havelis are elaborately designed, often incorporating intricate motifs and decorative flourishes. These elements add grandeur to the structure while maintaining symmetry and balance.

Integration of Art and Architecture:

The frescoes and decorative elements seamlessly integrate with the overall architectural design of the havelis. They adorn walls, ceilings, entrances, and courtyards, creating a visual experience that is both harmonious and awe-inspiring. Each element—whether a painted wall, carved jharokha, or ornamental pillar—reflects a meticulous effort to create beauty and meaning in every corner of the haveli.

Cultural Significance

The frescoes and decorative elements of Mandawa's havelis stand as a testament to the region's rich artistic traditions and the prosperity of its merchant class. They tell stories of history, religion, and changing times while offering a glimpse into the cultural and social life of Rajasthan's golden age. Today, these elements draw tourists, historians, and art lovers alike, preserving the legacy of the Shekhawati region for future generations.

Functional and Aesthetic Integration

The use of materials and the architectural features not only served practical climate considerations but also added to the aesthetic charm of the havelis.

- The lime-coated walls provided a perfect base for fresco paintings, which became a prominent cultural feature of Mandawa's havelis.

- Sandstone facades with carved arches, jharokhas, and ornamental pillars created an impressive visual identity while also providing shade and ventilation.

5.4 Materials and Climate Considerations

The havelis were constructed using local materials like sandstone, lime plaster, and bricks. The thick walls helped insulate the interiors against the intense heat of the desert, keeping the rooms cool in summer and warm in winter. The use of jharokhas, ventilators, and courtyards promoted cross-ventilation, a crucial design element for desert dwellings.

The roofs often featured flat terraces or small domes, serving as spaces for gatherings or enjoying cooler evening breezes. The entrances were grand, with massive gateways (*pols*) leading into the inner courtyards, signifying the status and prestige of the owners.

The construction of havelis in Mandawa primarily relied on locally available materials, which were both cost-effective and sustainable. These materials contributed to the longevity of the structures and their ability to withstand the region's harsh climate.

- **Sandstone**: Sandstone, a locally abundant material, was extensively used in constructing the walls, facades, and decorative elements. It is durable and naturally insulating, making it ideal for withstanding both scorching heat and occasional sandstorms.

- **Lime Plaster**: The walls of the havelis were coated with lime plaster, which acted as a natural coolant and gave the frescoes a smooth and bright surface. Lime also helped regulate humidity, making the interiors comfortable.

- **Bricks**: Locally made baked bricks were used for the main walls and partitions. The thickness of the walls helped in maintaining cooler indoor temperatures during summer and provided insulation in winter.

- **Wood**: Intricately carved wooden doors, windows, and balconies (jharokhas) were made from seasoned wood. The use of wood was strategic, as it allowed for ventilation while also adding aesthetic value.

- **Natural Pigments**: Frescoes on the walls were painted using natural pigments derived from minerals, plants, and stones. These colors not only gave vibrant life to the paintings but also withstood the test of time and environmental factors.

Symbol of Cultural Heritage

The havelis of Mandawa stand as a symbol of the prosperous merchant culture of the region and their appreciation for art, architecture, and aesthetics. These structures not only served as luxurious homes but also as canvases for artisans to showcase their skills. Today, these havelis attract tourists, historians, and art lovers from across the world, offering a glimpse into Rajasthan's glorious past. The havelis of Mandawa showcase a perfect blend of artistry, functionality, and environmental sensitivity. The thoughtful use of materials like sandstone, lime plaster, and wood, combined with climate-responsive features such as thick walls, courtyards, and jali work, highlights the ingenuity of traditional Rajasthani architecture. These timeless structures continue to inspire modern sustainable design while offering a glimpse into the region's rich cultural and architectural heritage.

5.5 Frescoes and Murals: Overview

The frescoes in Mandawa havelis are a distinct **wall painting style** where pigments are applied on a freshly plastered surface. This technique ensures that the colors penetrate the plaster, making the artwork long-lasting. The murals were created by skilled artisans, often local craftsmen, commissioned by the wealthy merchant families to adorn their homes. These paintings are the epitome of Shekhawati's artistic heritage.

Themes in Frescoes and Murals

The frescoes in Mandawa's havelis are known for their diversity of themes, ranging from religious stories to depictions of local life, and even scenes influenced by European and modern inventions of the time.

1. Religious Themes:

- **Hindu Mythology**: Many of the frescoes depict scenes from Hindu mythology, particularly the **Ramayana** and **Mahabharata**. These include **epic battles**, **divine interventions**, and portraits of **gods and goddesses** such as Krishna, Shiva, and Ganesha. For example, scenes of **Krishna's Raas Leela** (dance with the gopis) are common, reflecting devotion and cultural significance.

- **Portraits of Deities**: The frescoes often feature large, vibrant portraits of Hindu gods and goddesses, painted in exquisite detail. These images were both decorative and held spiritual significance, acting as blessings for the home and its inhabitants.

2. Rajput and Mughal Influences:

- **Royal Portraits**: Many frescoes in Mandawa depict **Rajput rulers** and **Mughal emperors**, adorned in elaborate attire and seated on thrones. These images emphasize the cultural exchange between Rajasthan's Rajputana heritage and the Mughal dynasty.

- **War Scenes**: Some frescoes depict battle scenes between **Rajput warriors** and their enemies, showcasing the bravery and valor of the Rajput kings. These murals often feature warriors on horseback, elephants in battle, and grand military parades.

3. Everyday Life:

- **Domestic and Social Life**: The frescoes also capture scenes from everyday life, providing a fascinating glimpse into the social customs, attire, and lifestyle of the people of the time. These murals often depict women engaged in household activities, men conducting business or relaxing, and village scenes with markets, festivals, and celebrations.

- **Trades and Professions**: The frescoes provide a visual record of the various professions in the region, including **carpenters**, **blacksmiths**, **potters**, and **textile traders**. The representation of different trades highlights the importance of craftsmanship and commerce in Mandawa's society.

- **Musicians and Dancers**: The vibrant culture of Rajasthan is also depicted through frescoes that portray **traditional musicians** and **folk dancers**. These murals often show performances during festivals and celebrations, underscoring the region's rich cultural traditions.

4. European and Modern Influences:

- **Colonial Influence**: As trade expanded during the British colonial period, European influences began to appear in the frescoes. Merchants who had traveled to Europe or were influenced by Western culture commissioned frescoes depicting **British officials**, **Victorian architecture**, and **European fashion**. This marked a unique fusion of East and West in the art of Mandawa.

- **Depiction of Modern Technology**: In the late 19th and early 20th centuries, the frescoes began to feature representations of **modern inventions** such as **trains**, **cars**, **telephones**, and **gramophones**. These elements reflect the changing world and the embrace of technological advancements by the wealthy merchant class. It's quite remarkable to see paintings of trains and bicycles next to traditional mythological figures!

- **Satirical and Humorous Scenes**: Some frescoes, influenced by European satirical art, depict humorous scenes or parodies, particularly of British colonial officials. These murals serve as subtle commentaries on the changing socio-political landscape of the time.

5. Architectural Frescoes:

- **Frescoes on Walls and Ceilings**: The walls and ceilings of Mandawa's havelis are often covered with elaborate frescoes. Ceilings in particular were decorated with **floral patterns**, **geometric designs**, or mythological scenes that could be admired from below.

- **Decorative Borders and Frames**: Many frescoes are framed with ornate decorative borders, often painted in gold, deep red, or blue. These borders add to the visual richness of the murals and help create a cohesive design across entire walls or rooms.

5.6 Techniques and Materials Used

The frescoes of Mandawa were created using the **"fresco buono" technique**, where pigments were applied onto wet lime plaster, allowing the colors to seep into the surface and become part of the wall as it dried. This method ensured that the murals remained vibrant and durable for centuries.

- **Natural Pigments**: The colors used in the frescoes were derived from **natural sources** like minerals, plants, and stones. For example:

  - **Red** was made from iron oxide.

  - **Blue** came from indigo or lapis lazuli.

  - **Yellow** was sourced from ochre.

  - **Green** was made from copper compounds.

  - **White** was lime, and **black** was often made from lamp soot.

- **Intricate Detailing**: The artisans used thin brushes made of animal hair to create fine details, especially in the depiction of human figures, animals, and clothing. The meticulous craftsmanship is evident in the precision of the lines and the vibrancy of the colors, despite the passage of time.

5.7 Cultural Significance of Frescoes

The frescoes of Mandawa hold immense cultural and historical importance, representing a visual record of the region's past. They are a direct reflection of the town's socio-economic and cultural life during the peak of Shekhawati's prosperity.

1. Patronage of the Merchant Class:

The frescoes were commissioned by **wealthy merchants** who sought to display their prosperity and cultural sophistication through art. These merchants were not only patrons of architecture but also of visual arts, ensuring that their homes became canvases for master artists. The frescoes were a way for these families to showcase their status while also contributing to the town's cultural landscape.

2. Preservation of Local Culture:

The frescoes are invaluable for the way they preserve the local culture, customs, and traditions of Mandawa and the broader Shekhawati region. Scenes of Rajasthani life, including clothing, festivities, and religious rituals, are immortalized in these paintings, offering insight into how people lived, celebrated, and worked centuries ago.

3. Blending of Cultures:

The influence of European elements in the frescoes marks the unique blending of cultures that took place in Mandawa due to the merchants' interactions with British and other Western traders. This fusion of Indian tradition with European modernity is a hallmark of the Shekhawati frescoes and makes them distinct from other forms of Indian art.

Current State and Conservation Challenges:

While the frescoes of Mandawa are priceless pieces of art, many have unfortunately deteriorated over time due to neglect, exposure to the elements, and a lack of proper maintenance. As many of the havelis have been abandoned or left in disrepair, the frescoes have suffered damage from water seepage, dust, and general wear and tear.

- **Restoration Efforts**: Some efforts have been made to restore these murals, particularly in havelis that have been converted into **heritage hotels** or **museums**. These restoration projects are crucial to preserving this unique cultural and artistic heritage for future generations.

- **Tourism's Role**: The rise of tourism in Mandawa has also helped draw attention to the importance of preserving the frescoes. Tourists, art historians, and cultural enthusiasts are increasingly visiting Mandawa to admire its havelis and frescoes, which has led to more local interest in their preservation.

Conclusion:

The frescoes and murals of Mandawa are not merely decorative elements of the town's havelis; they are a vibrant testament to the town's **historical, cultural, and artistic significance**. From mythological tales and royal portraits to depictions of modern technology and European influence, these paintings are a rich tapestry of the region's heritage. As we look to the future, it's crucial that efforts continue to preserve these frescoes so that Mandawa's legacy as the "open-air art gallery" of Rajasthan remains alive for generations to come.

6.MANDAWA FORT

Mandawa Fort is one of the most prominent landmarks in the town of Mandawa, located in the Shekhawati region of Rajasthan. This fort, built in the mid-18th century, stands as a testament to the rich cultural heritage of the area and reflects the grandeur of Rajput architecture. Over the years, Mandawa Fort has played a crucial role in the town's history and is now a significant attraction, drawing tourists with its magnificent architecture, intricate artwork, and historical significance.

6.1 History of Mandawa Fort

The construction of Mandawa Fort began in 1755 under Thakur Nawal Singh, the ruler of Mandawa and a descendant of Rao Shekhaji, the founder of the Shekhawati region. Thakur Nawal Singh was a Rajput ruler who established the town of Mandawa, strategically located on an ancient trade route that connected India to the Middle East and Central Asia. The fort was built as both a defensive stronghold and a residence for the ruling family, designed to protect the region from potential invaders and provide a secure base for the growing prosperity of the town.

During its time, Mandawa became a hub for wealthy traders and merchants who built elaborate havelis around the fort, transforming the town into a prosperous center for commerce and culture. The fort played a central role in the town's development, and it also served as a place of administration and governance for the rulers of the region.

6.2 Architecture of Mandawa Fort

The architecture of Mandawa Fort is a fine example of Rajput military and residential design, with features that reflect the fort's dual purpose as both a defensive structure and a palatial residence. The fort was designed to withstand attacks while also offering comfort and luxury to its inhabitants.

1. Fortifications and Defensive Design:

Thick Walls and Bastions: The fort is surrounded by thick stone walls, typical of Rajput forts, designed to protect the fort from external threats. These walls are punctuated by bastions and turrets at strategic points, allowing guards to keep watch and defend against any attacks. The strong fortifications highlight the military significance of Mandawa Fort during its early years.

Gates (Pols): The fort is accessed through a grand entrance gate (or pol), which served both as a defensive structure and as a statement of the power of the ruling family. The gate is adorned with decorative elements, including frescoes, carvings, and a metal-spiked door, designed to protect the fort from elephant charges during enemy sieges.

Defensive Layout: The layout of the fort follows a strategic defensive design, with multiple courtyards, narrow passages, and watchtowers that allowed the rulers to keep a close eye on the surrounding area. The fort's elevated position on a small hill also gave it a vantage point, providing an advantage during potential attacks.

2. Residential and Palatial Features:

Palatial Rooms: While the outer walls and fortifications were built with defense in mind, the interior of the fort is a striking contrast, designed to offer luxury and comfort to the royal family. The fort's interior rooms are decorated with intricate frescoes, mirror work, and elaborate Rajasthani carvings that display the region's artistic traditions.

Darbar Hall: One of the most notable features of the fort is the Darbar Hall (Royal Courtroom), where the ruler would hold court and meet with officials and dignitaries. The hall is beautifully decorated with frescoes depicting scenes from Hindu mythology, Rajput history, and the royal lineage. The ceilings and pillars are often adorned with gold leaf and intricate paintings, reflecting the opulence of the time.

Private Chambers: The private chambers of the royal family were designed with luxury in mind, featuring jharokhas (ornate balconies), pillared corridors, and intricately decorated ceilings. These rooms often have access to private courtyards and terraces that provided ventilation and privacy to the royal family. The zenana (women's quarters) was a secluded area where the women of the household lived and conducted their daily activities in privacy, in keeping with the customs of the time.

Courtyards and Gardens: Like many Rajput forts, Mandawa Fort features open courtyards that acted as central spaces for social gatherings, celebrations, and ceremonies. These courtyards are surrounded by rooms on all sides and offer beautiful views of the gardens and surroundings. In addition to the courtyards, the fort includes terraced gardens that provide a tranquil space amid the grand architecture.

3. Frescoes and Decorative Artwork:

Frescoes: One of the most striking features of Mandawa Fort is the presence of exquisite frescoes that cover the walls and ceilings of the rooms and courtyards. These frescoes depict scenes from Hindu mythology, Rajput battles, historical events, and everyday life. The use of natural pigments and the detailed artistry make these frescoes some of the finest examples of Shekhawati's renowned fresco tradition.

Mirror Work: In some rooms, mirror inlay work (called Sheesh Mahal style) was used to enhance the grandeur of the fort's interiors. The mirrors reflect light, creating a dazzling effect that adds to the opulence of the royal chambers.

Floral and Geometric Patterns: The fort also features floral motifs, geometric designs, and arabesque patterns that are characteristic of Rajput and Mughal architecture. These designs are incorporated into the arches, pillars, and window frames, enhancing the beauty of the structure.

6.3 The Role of Mandawa Fort in the Region

1. Center of Power:

During its early years, Mandawa Fort served as the administrative and military center of the Mandawa thikana (feudal estate) within the Shekhawati region. The fort was a place where the rulers conducted governance, resolved disputes, and managed the region's growing economy. Its strategic location on a major trade route contributed to Mandawa's prosperity, as the fort helped maintain peace and security for traders and travelers passing through the area.

2. Patronage of Arts and Culture:

The fort became a focal point for the arts and culture in the region. The rulers of Mandawa were patrons of the arts and encouraged the creation of the frescoes that adorn both the fort and the havelis surrounding it. This tradition of patronage led to the flourishing of art in the Shekhawati region, and the fort played a key role in fostering this artistic movement.

3. Role in Trade and Commerce:

As Mandawa was a prominent stop on the trade route between Delhi and Gujarat, the fort also served as a center for commerce. Traders and merchants would often stop in Mandawa to conduct business, and the fort helped oversee the region's trade, ensuring the safety of goods and travelers. The wealth accumulated from trade contributed to the development of the town and the construction of the grand havelis that surround the fort.

Current State of Mandawa Fort

Today, Mandawa Fort has been transformed into a heritage hotel, offering visitors a chance to experience the grandeur and opulence of Rajasthan's royal past. The fort has been carefully restored to preserve its architectural and artistic features, allowing guests to stay in rooms that once housed royalty.

Heritage Hotel: As a heritage hotel, Mandawa Fort offers a unique blend of modern amenities and historical charm. Guests can explore the grand courtyards, marvel at the frescoes, and dine in rooms that have retained their original decor. The fort's transformation into a hotel has helped preserve its legacy and allows visitors to immerse themselves in the history and culture of Rajasthan.

Tourist Attraction: The fort is also a popular tourist attraction, drawing visitors from around the world who are eager to experience the history and architecture of Mandawa. The fort's frescoes, intricate carvings, and panoramic views of the surrounding town make it a must-visit destination in Shekhawati.

Cultural Events: In addition to being a heritage hotel, the fort hosts cultural events, including traditional Rajasthani folk performances, royal-themed dinners, and celebrations of regional festivals. These events allow visitors to experience the rich cultural heritage of Mandawa in a royal setting.

6.4 Significance of Mandawa Fort

Mandawa Fort holds immense historical, architectural, and cultural significance for the Shekhawati region. It stands as a symbol of Rajput grandeur and Rajasthan's rich heritage, reflecting the power and influence of the rulers who built it. The fort's frescoes and architectural features also serve as a visual record of the region's artistic traditions, making it an important part of India's cultural legacy.

Architectural Legacy: The fort represents the fusion of Rajput and Mughal architectural styles, showcasing the craftsmanship of the artisans who built and decorated it. Its strong fortifications and luxurious interiors embody the dual nature of Rajput forts as both defensive strongholds and palatial residences.

Cultural Heritage: Mandawa Fort has played a key role in the preservation and promotion of Shekhawati's artistic heritage. The frescoes that adorn its walls and the surrounding havelis are a reflection of the town's cultural and artistic vibrancy.

Chhatris, also known as cenotaphs, are an iconic feature of Rajasthani architecture, particularly in the Shekhawati region, including Mandawa. These structures were built to commemorate Rajput royalty, noblemen, and influential figures, often serving as memorials for the deceased. In Mandawa, chhatris are significant not only for their architectural beauty but also for the cultural and historical narratives they represent. They stand as symbols of honor and remembrance, and their intricate designs showcase the artistic excellence of the time.

Let's explore chhatris in detail, focusing on their architectural features, historical significance, and cultural role in Mandawa.

1. What Are Chhatris?

The term "chhatri" literally means "umbrella" in Hindi, referring to the domed shape of these structures, which resembles a protective canopy. Chhatris were originally designed as cenotaphs or memorials to honor notable individuals, particularly kings, warriors, or wealthy patrons. Unlike mausoleums, chhatris are not always tombs; rather, they are monuments built to honor the deceased.

In Mandawa and other parts of Shekhawati, chhatris were built to memorialize Rajput rulers, merchants, and other prominent members of society. These cenotaphs often commemorate the lives of individuals by celebrating their deeds and legacy in the form of a grand architectural structure.

2. Architectural Features of Chhatris

The architecture of chhatris is a perfect blend of Rajputana and Mughal styles, reflecting the fusion of artistic traditions in Rajasthan. These structures are distinguished by their domes, pillared pavilions, and elaborate carvings, making them visually striking elements of the landscape.

a. Domes and Canopies:

The most distinctive feature of a chhatri is its domed roof, which is often intricately carved and adorned with decorative elements. The umbrella-shaped dome serves as a symbolic representation of protection, shielding the memory of the deceased.

Chhatris may have single domes or multiple smaller domes (in larger structures), depending on the prominence of the individual being commemorated. The domes are typically supported by pillars and are topped with a kalash (an ornamental finial) that adds to the aesthetic appeal of the structure.

b. Pillared Pavilions:

Chhatris are often constructed as open-air pavilions, supported by carved stone pillars that form the structure's framework. These pillars, usually made of sandstone or marble, are intricately carved with motifs such as floral patterns, geometric designs, and mythological figures. The pillars not only serve a structural purpose but also enhance the visual grace of the chhatris. They create a sense of openness, allowing natural light to filter through, which casts beautiful shadows and adds to the overall aesthetic.

c. Base and Platform:

Most chhatris are built on raised platforms or plinths, which are often carved or engraved with intricate designs. These platforms elevate the structure, giving it a sense of grandeur and importance. The steps leading up to the platform signify the journey toward the afterlife or ascension to a higher realm.

The base of the chhatri often features elaborate stonework, with decorative borders and panels that depict scenes from Rajput history, mythology, or nature.

d. Frescoes and Decorative Elements:

In many cases, especially in Shekhawati's chhatris, the interior walls and ceilings are adorned with frescoes. These frescoes often depict scenes from Hindu epics like the Ramayana or Mahabharata, along with images of gods and goddesses, royal portraits, and battle scenes.

The frescoes inside chhatris are similar to those found in Mandawa's havelis, reflecting the artistic traditions of the Shekhawati region. The paintings also capture the local customs, festivals, and rituals associated with death and the afterlife.

e. Variety of Designs:

While most chhatris follow a similar architectural design, their size, grandeur, and decoration vary based on the status and wealth of the individual being commemorated. Some chhatris are simple and modest, while others are grand and elaborately designed with multiple domes and ornate carvings.

3. Symbolism and Cultural Significance

The chhatris of Mandawa are not merely architectural marvels; they carry deep symbolic meaning and serve important cultural functions.

a. Honor and Legacy:

The primary function of chhatris is to honor the memory of the deceased. In the case of Rajput rulers or wealthy merchants, these structures were built to commemorate their achievements, bravery, and contributions to society. The grandeur of a chhatri often reflects the status and legacy of the person it honors.

By constructing these cenotaphs, the family or community ensures that the memory of the deceased is preserved for future generations, embodying the values of respect, loyalty, and devotion.

b. Rituals and Commemorations:

Chhatris also serve as places for rituals and ceremonies honoring the dead. Families often visit these memorials on death anniversaries to perform rites and offer prayers for the soul of the departed. These ceremonies reinforce the cultural belief in ancestral reverence and the afterlife.

The construction of a chhatri after a person's death is also tied to the belief in moksha (spiritual liberation), a concept in Hinduism where the soul is freed from the cycle of birth and death.

c. Chhatris as Symbols of Valor:

In the case of Rajput rulers and warriors, chhatris often represent bravery and valor. Many chhatris are dedicated to warriors who died in battle, serving as memorials to their sacrifice. The martial traditions of Rajasthan are reflected in the grandness of the chhatris, which often feature carvings of warriors on horseback or scenes of battle.

d. Architectural Legacy:

Chhatris contribute to the architectural legacy of Rajasthan, particularly in the Shekhawati region. They demonstrate the craftsmanship and artistry of local artisans and are a key feature of the region's heritage. Over time, chhatris have become not only places of remembrance but also important tourist attractions, drawing visitors who admire their beauty and historical significance.

4. Notable Chhatris in Mandawa

Mandawa, with its rich heritage, is home to several notable chhatris, each reflecting the town's history and culture. Many of these chhatris were built by wealthy merchant families or in honor of Rajput rulers, and they are located throughout the town and its surrounding areas.

a. Chhatris of Thakur Families:

Several chhatris in Mandawa commemorate the Thakur family, the ruling Rajput clan of the region. These chhatris are often located near the fort or within designated family areas. They are typically grand, with intricate carvings and large domes, celebrating the valor and leadership of the family members.

b. Merchant Chhatris:

Wealthy merchants, who made their fortunes through trade in Mandawa, also commissioned chhatris for their deceased family members. These structures often feature frescoes and artwork that reflect both their Rajasthani heritage and the influence of the trade routes they operated on, with scenes of travelers, camels, and caravans depicted on the walls.

c. Shekhawati's Unique Frescoed Chhatris:

Some of the most interesting chhatris in Mandawa and the surrounding Shekhawati region are those decorated with frescoes. These frescoed chhatris blend the artistic traditions of the region with memorial architecture, creating a unique cultural artifact. The frescoes in these chhatris often depict mythological scenes, historical events, and portraits of the deceased, offering a visual narrative of the individual's life and achievements.

7. HAVELI

7.1 Murmuria Haveli

Murmuria Haveli is one of the most famous havelis in Mandawa, known for its eclectic and visually striking frescoes that blend traditional Rajasthani themes with colonial-era influences.

Architectural Features:

Frescoes: The frescoes in Murmuria Haveli are unique for depicting modern European elements, such as images of trains, cars, and even bicycles, alongside British soldiers and Indian royalty. One of the most famous frescoes here is of Jawaharlal Nehru riding a horse with the Indian flag in hand, a nod to the Indian independence movement.

Blend of Styles: The haveli's architecture reflects a fusion of Rajput and colonial styles, with traditional arched windows, pillared balconies, and modern imagery painted across its walls.

Decorative Jharokhas: The facade features ornate jharokhas (balconies), typical of Rajasthani architecture, offering a glimpse into the interplay between private and public spaces within the haveli.

Murmuria Haveli stands out for its ability to blend traditional Indian craftsmanship with global influences, reflecting the cosmopolitan outlook of the merchants who commissioned it.

7.2 Gulab Rai Ladia Haveli

The **Gulab Rai Ladia Haveli** is often regarded as one of the **most beautiful havelis** in Mandawa. Built in the 19th century, it exemplifies the **artistic and architectural opulence** of Shekhawati's merchant class.

Architectural Features:

- **Exquisite Frescoes**: The haveli is particularly renowned for its **beautiful frescoes**, which are painted in vibrant colors and depict **mythological scenes**, **erotic themes**, and **historical episodes**. The frescoes in Gulab Rai Ladia Haveli are considered some of the finest examples of **Shekhawati art**, with delicate brushwork and attention to detail.

- **Intricate Carvings**: The **entrance gate** and **windows** feature intricate **wood and stone carvings**, adding to the decorative richness of the haveli. The wooden doors are especially noteworthy for their fine craftsmanship.

- **Courtyard Architecture**: Like many havelis, Gulab Rai Ladia Haveli is centered around a **courtyard**, providing ventilation and privacy for the residents. The courtyard is lined with **arched pillars**, and the rooms open into this central space.

This haveli's architecture is a testament to the **aesthetic refinement** of the Shekhawati merchants and showcases the blending of **art, architecture, and functionality**.

7.3 Jhunjhunwala Haveli

Jhunjhunwala Haveli is another prominent example of Mandawa's architectural grandeur. It is known for its vast size and the extensive use of frescoes depicting Hindu gods and goddesses.

Architectural Features:

- **Religious Frescoes**: The frescoes in Jhunjhunwala Haveli are primarily focused on **religious themes**. They depict various deities such as **Lord Krishna**, **Vishnu**, and scenes from the **Ramayana** and **Mahabharata**, reflecting the spiritual inclinations of its owners.

- **Ornate Doorways**: The haveli's entrances and doorways are decorated with **ornate arches** and **carvings**, adding a sense of grandiosity to the building. The doors themselves are made of finely carved **wood**, showcasing local craftsmanship.

- **Grand Facade**: The exterior of the haveli is adorned with **floral motifs**, **geometric patterns**, and **mythological figures**, which give the structure a highly decorative appearance.

- **Courtyard and Pillars**: The haveli features the **traditional Shekhawati layout**, with a **central courtyard** surrounded by rooms. The courtyard is framed by **pillared corridors**, adding to the sense of openness and space.

The **intricate religious art** and **grand architectural layout** of Jhunjhunwala Haveli make it a symbol of both **piety** and **prestige**

7.4 Goenka Double Haveli

The **Goenka Double Haveli** is one of the most striking examples of **Rajasthani haveli architecture** in Mandawa. It was built by the **Goenka family**, one of the wealthiest merchant families in the region, and is notable for its **double facade** and extensive frescoes.

Architectural Features:

- **Double Facade**: As the name suggests, the haveli has a **double facade**, meaning that it has two separate front-facing facades, each intricately decorated. This gives the haveli a larger-than-life appearance, and it is one of the few examples of such a design in Mandawa.

- **Extensive Frescoes**: The walls of the Goenka Double Haveli are covered with elaborate frescoes, depicting a variety of themes, including **mythological stories**, **scenes of royal processions**, **British colonial influence**, and **everyday life**. The frescoes also include **images of animals** like elephants and horses, symbolizing power and prosperity.

- **Intricate Arches and Jharokhas**: The haveli's architectural design includes **high arches** and **jharokhas** (projecting windows), which are carved with delicate floral and geometric patterns. These architectural elements are typical of **Rajasthani havelis** and add to the haveli's grandeur.

- **Courtyard Layout**: The haveli follows the **traditional layout** of a large **central courtyard**, which is framed by rooms and open corridors on multiple sides.

Goenka Double Haveli stands out for its **lavish scale**, reflecting the **wealth** and **influence** of the Goenka family in Mandawa.

7.5 Hanuman Prasad Goenka Haveli

Another architectural masterpiece in Mandawa is the **Hanuman Prasad Goenka Haveli**, known for its **vivid frescoes** that cover its walls and ceilings.

Architectural Features:

- **Frescoes of Hindu Deities**: The frescoes in this haveli primarily depict **Hindu gods and goddesses**, including **Lord Shiva** on his bull **Nandi**, **Lord Krishna** playing the flute, and **Lord Vishnu** with his consort **Lakshmi**. These images not only serve as religious symbols but also showcase the artistic talent of the local painters.

- **Colonial Influences**: Interestingly, the haveli also features some **European influences**, such as frescoes of **British officers** and scenes of **Western lifestyle**, including images of men in top hats and scenes of modern transportation like **trains** and **cars**.

- **Open Courtyard**: Like other havelis, Hanuman Prasad Goenka Haveli is built around an **open courtyard**, which ensures good ventilation and provides a space for family gatherings and religious ceremonies.

- **Elegant Arches and Jharokhas**: The haveli's facade is characterized by **arched windows** and **projecting balconies** with beautifully carved **railings**, typical of **Rajasthani architecture**.

The **rich frescoes** and the **fusion of cultural themes** in Hanuman Prasad Goenka Haveli make it a prime example of how **Shekhawati merchants** blended **local traditions** with influences from the **outside world**.

7.6 The Mohan Lal Saraf Haveli

Mohan Lal Saraf Haveli is another renowned haveli in Mandawa, showcasing the opulence and artistic achievements of the merchant class.

Architectural Features:

- **Elaborate Frescoes**: The frescoes in this haveli are incredibly detailed, covering themes from **mythology**, **social customs**, and **historic events**. The artwork is known for its **use of natural colors** and the fine detailing in depicting human figures, animals, and flora.

- **Courtyard Design**: The haveli follows the **Shekhawati courtyard style**, with rooms surrounding the central open space. The courtyard is typically used for family gatherings and religious rituals.

- **Grand Facade**: The facade of the haveli is richly decorated with **ornamental brackets**, **arches**, and **jharokhas**, giving it an imposing yet beautiful appearance.

7.7 Chokhani Double Haveli

- **Overview**: Built by the wealthy Chokhani family, this haveli showcases the family's opulence and taste.

- **Features**: The exterior and interior walls are adorned with vivid murals depicting **mythological themes** and **floral motifs**. One notable feature is the depiction of **Krishna**, surrounded by his female devotees, which embodies both artistry and devotion.

- **Artistic Highlights**: The intricately painted ceilings display geometric designs intertwined with vibrant floral patterns, showcasing the skills of the artisans.

Sethani Ka Johara

- **Overview**: This haveli is known for its elaborate frescoes and rich decorative elements.

- **Features**: The walls are covered with scenes from daily life, including **weddings, festivals**, and **marketplaces**. The frescoes also depict traditional Rajasthani dance forms, capturing the vibrant cultural life of the era.

- **Artistic Highlights**: The bright colors and dynamic compositions of the frescoes provide a lively portrayal of the social customs and traditions of Mandawa.

7.8 Kedia Dola Haveli

- **Overview**: This haveli is recognized for its beautiful murals reflecting both local and Mughal influences.

- **Features**: The paintings include scenes of **nature**, **wildlife**, and **mythological stories**, with intricate details that draw the viewer's eye.

- **Artistic Highlights**: The use of soft pastels and detailed animal motifs create a serene ambiance, showcasing the artisans' ability to blend realism with artistic imagination.

7.9 Haveli of Gulab Rai Ladia

- **Overview**: This haveli stands out for its grand architecture and detailed frescoes.

- **Features**: The havelis feature vibrant murals that narrate various themes, including **love stories**, **royal exploits**, and **scenes of nature**.

- **Artistic Highlights**: The frescoes are notable for their vivid color palette and intricate detailing, making them a focal point of attraction for visitors.

8.CULTURAL SIGNIFICANCE OF THE PAINTINGS

The paintings in Mandawa's havelis carry immense cultural significance, serving as windows into the past and reflecting the region's rich heritage.

8.1 Artistic Styles of Frescoes

The frescoes in Mandawa's havelis exhibit a variety of artistic styles that reflect both traditional Indian art forms and the influences of various cultural exchanges over time.

Traditional Techniques

- **Fresco Secco**: Most frescoes in Mandawa are created using the fresco secco technique, where dry plaster is painted over with natural pigments. This method allows the colors to retain their vibrancy for centuries. Unlike true fresco (buon fresco), where colors are applied to wet plaster, fresco secco offers greater flexibility in design and detail.

- **Natural Pigments**: The artists used natural materials for pigments, such as minerals (for blues and- greens), plant extracts (for reds and yellows), and even gold and silver leaf to add a touch of opulence. The use of these materials is a testament to the craftsmanship and resourcefulness of the artisans.

Design Elements

- **Intricate Detailing**: The havelis showcase an array of detailed designs, including floral patterns, geometric shapes, and mythological motifs. These elements create a rich tapestry that covers walls and ceilings, transforming spaces into immersive experiences.

- **Borders and Frames**: The use of decorative borders and frames around the main scenes not only enhances the visual appeal but also defines the narratives depicted in the murals. These borders often feature intricate designs that connect different scenes.

8.2 Themes Depicted in the Paintings

The frescoes of Mandawa are distinguished by their diverse them-es, which range from mythological narratives to depictions of daily life.

Mythological Narratives

- **Hindu Deities**: Many murals feature prominent Hindu deities, such as Krishna, Rama, and Durga, often depicted in various mythological scenes. These images serve not only a decorative purpose but also convey religious sentiments and cultural values.

- **Epic Tales**: Frescoes illustrating stories from the **Ramayana** and **Mahabharata** are common. These narratives not only entertain but also impart moral lessons and cultural teachings.

Royal Life and Valor

- **Warriors and Battles**: Scenes showcasing Rajput warriors in battle, often adorned with elaborate armor and weapons, emphasize the martial culture of the time. These paintings celebrate bravery, honor, and the valor of the Rajput rulers.

- **Hunting Scenes**: Frescoes depicting hunting expeditions were popular, illustrating the nobility's engagement with nature and their prowess in hunting. These scenes often portray the royal elite in grand attire, accompanied by huntsmen and animals.

Floral and Geometric Patterns

- **Nature Motifs**: Floral designs are prevalent throughout the havelis, symbolizing fertility, beauty, and nature. These patterns often incorporate local flora, enhancing the connection to the surrounding environment.

- **Geometric Designs**: The geometric motifs, often intertwined with floral patterns, add a layer of sophistication and structure to the compositions, reflecting the influence of Persian and Mughal art.

Daily Life and Customs

- **Social Life**: Many frescoes depict scenes from everyday life, showcasing traditional Rajasthani customs, festivals, and community gatherings. These paintings provide a snapshot of the cultural practices and social norms of the time.

- **Craftsmanship and Trades**: Some murals illustrate local artisans at work, highlighting the region's rich craft traditions, including textiles, pottery, and jewelry-making. These representations celebrate the skills and livelihoods of the local community.

Colonial Influence

- **Western Themes**: With the advent of British colonialism, some havelis began to incorporate Western elements in their frescoes, such as horse-drawn carriages, colonial architecture, and European-style clothing. This blend of styles reflects the changing dynamics of trade and cultural exchange during this period.

9. DOCUMENTS AND PRESERVATION OF HERITAGE

9.1 Historical Documentation

- **Cultural Context**: The frescoes provide insights into the socio-economic and cultural dynamics of Mandawa during its prosperous era. They capture the values, beliefs, and traditions of the community, making them invaluable historical documents.

- **Artistic Legacy**: These artworks represent a unique blend of various artistic influences, documenting the evolution of Indian art in response to cultural and social changes. They exemplify the craftsmanship and creativity of the artists who dedicated their skills to these works.

9.2 Preservation of Heritage

- **Cultural Identity**: The frescoes are an essential aspect of Rajasthan's cultural identity. They embody the region's artistic traditions and contribute to the understanding of Indian history and culture.

- **Tourism and Education**: The rich artistic heritage of Mandawa has turned the town into a significant tourist destination. The frescoes draw visitors, scholars, and art enthusiasts, providing opportunities for education and cultural exchange.

9.3 Community Connection
- **Social Reflection**: The paintings connect the present generation with their historical roots, fostering a sense of pride and identity within the local community. They serve as a reminder of the town's legacy and the achievements of its ancestors.

9.4 Preservation Efforts
Despite their significance, the frescoes face various threats, including natural wear and tear, urban development, and climatic changes. Ongoing preservation efforts are crucial to maintaining the integrity of these artworks.

9.5 Restoration Projects
- **Conservation Initiatives**: Organizations such as the Indian National Trust for Art and Cultural Heritage (INTACH) have undertaken restoration projects to preserve the frescoes. These efforts include stabilizing the structures, repairing damaged frescoes, and using non-invasive techniques to clean and restore the paintings.

- **Government Support**: Local governments and heritage organizations are increasingly recognizing the importance of preserving Mandawa's architectural heritage. Initiatives are being implemented to promote awareness and fund restoration efforts.

9.6 Community Involvement
- **Local Engagement**: Engaging the local community in preservation efforts is vital. Training programs for artisans and local residents can empower them to take an active role in safeguarding their cultural heritage.

- **Educational Outreach**: Workshops and educational programs can raise awareness about the significance of these artworks, fostering a sense of ownership and responsibility among the local population.

9.7 Tourism Management
- **Sustainable Tourism**: Promoting responsible tourism practices can help mitigate the impact of visitor footfall on the frescoes. Developing guidelines for visitors and enhancing visitor education can ensure that the artworks are treated with respect and care.

Mandawa, like many other historic towns in India, faces a variety of urban issues that stem from a combination of rapid development, tourism growth, and the challenges of preserving its cultural heritage. While Mandawa's rich architectural and artistic heritage has made it a major tourist destination, it also brings with it certain pressures that the town is struggling to manage effectively. Here are some of the major urban issues that Mandawa is currently facing:

Heritage Conservation and Preservation

One of the most pressing issues in Mandawa is the deterioration of its historic havelis, frescoes, and other heritage buildings due to neglect, weathering, and modernization pressures.

- **Lack of Maintenance**: Many of the havelis that once showcased exquisite frescoes and carvings are now in a state of disrepair. Owners of these havelis, who no longer reside in Mandawa or have shifted to modern homes, often do not invest in their maintenance. As a result, these historical buildings are left neglected, and many frescoes have faded or been damaged.

- **Unsustainable Tourism**: The influx of tourists has led to an increase in commercial activities, putting pressure on the historical infrastructure. Many heritage buildings are being modified or altered to accommodate modern needs, such as converting havelis into hotels, which sometimes leads to inappropriate renovations that compromise the integrity of the original architecture.

- **Lack of Skilled Conservation**: There is a shortage of skilled artisans and professionals who can properly restore the frescoes and architecture. This has led to improper restoration efforts that do more harm than good, sometimes altering the original aesthetic and cultural value of these sites.

9.8 Urbanization and Unplanned Development

Mandawa's growing reputation as a tourist destination has led to a rise in commercial activities and unplanned urban development, which negatively affects the town's character and infrastructure.

- **Modern Construction**: New construction, often without regard for the town's traditional aesthetic or architectural harmony, has begun to replace older structures. This haphazard development disrupts the visual landscape of the town, with new buildings often clashing with the town's historical identity.

- **Encroachment**: Illegal constructions and encroachments on public land, as well as unauthorized extensions of properties, are common in Mandawa. These encroachments block streets, cause traffic congestion, and undermine the original layout of the town.

- **Infrastructure Strain**: The existing infrastructure, including roads, water supply, and waste management systems, is unable to cope with the town's growing population and tourist traffic. This results in water shortages, poor sanitation, and overcrowding in certain areas, especially around tourist spots.

Tourism Pressure

While tourism is a key driver of Mandawa's economy, it also presents several challenges that the town is struggling to manage effectively.

- **Overtourism**: The surge in tourism, particularly during peak seasons, places enormous pressure on the town's infrastructure. Overcrowded streets, traffic congestion, and insufficient parking facilities are common issues. Tourist buses and vehicles often clog narrow streets, disrupting the daily life of local residents.

- **Environmental Degradation**: The increase in tourist numbers has led to issues such as littering, poor waste management, and the degradation of the environment. Improper waste disposal by hotels, restaurants, and tourists results in pollution, particularly in areas surrounding the havelis and heritage sites.

- **Cultural Erosion**: The commercialization of the town to cater to tourists sometimes leads to the commodification of local culture. Traditional ways of life, including crafts, art, and social customs, are sometimes simplified or altered to suit tourist expectations, leading to a loss of authenticity.

9.9 Lack of Infrastructure Development

Mandawa's infrastructure has not kept pace with its growing population and tourism sector, leading to several challenges that affect both residents and visitors.

- **Water Scarcity**: Mandawa, like much of Rajasthan, faces water scarcity due to its arid climate and limited water resources. The town's traditional water harvesting systems, such as step wells and baoris, are either in disuse or have been damaged over time. Increasing demand from hotels and other tourist facilities has exacerbated the water supply issue.

- **Roads and Transportation**: The road infrastructure in Mandawa is not equipped to handle heavy traffic, especially during peak tourist seasons. Narrow streets, combined with the presence of tourist buses and private vehicles, lead to traffic jams and poor road conditions.

- **Waste Management**: The town lacks an effective waste management system, leading to improper disposal of garbage in public areas. The accumulation of waste not only affects the town's aesthetic appeal but also creates health hazards for both residents and tourists.

9.10 Environmental Degradation

Environmental issues in Mandawa stem from a combination of urban growth, tourism, and climate challenges.

- **Desertification and Dust**: Being in the arid region of Rajasthan, Mandawa is prone to desertification, with dust storms and sand accumulation affecting the air quality and visibility. This also accelerates the deterioration of frescoes and historic buildings, which are exposed to dust and sand erosion.

- **Deforestation**: The loss of green cover around Mandawa, due to construction activities and agricultural expansion, has contributed to environmental imbalances, making the town more vulnerable to desert conditions and extreme weather.

- **Water Pollution**: The limited water sources in Mandawa, including groundwater, are often polluted due to improper disposal of sewage and industrial waste from small-scale industries and hotels. This poses a threat to both public health and the environment.

9.11 Migration and Depopulation

Mandawa has also seen significant migration patterns that have affected the town's social and economic fabric.

- **Out-Migration**: A significant number of local residents, particularly the younger generation, have moved to bigger cities in search of better economic opportunities, education, and jobs. This depopulation has left many havelis abandoned or underutilized, as there are fewer people to maintain them.

- **Population Imbalance**: The depopulation of locals is contrasted by the influx of seasonal workers and tourism-related employees who come to Mandawa during peak tourist seasons. This has led to a temporary population increase, putting additional pressure on the town's infrastructure during these periods.

9.12 Lack of Heritage Awareness and Community Involvement

A major challenge in Mandawa is the lack of awareness among the local population regarding the importance of heritage preservation.

- **Neglect of Heritage**: Many local residents, especially younger generations, often view the historical havelis as burdens rather than assets. The cost of maintaining these heritage properties is high, and without government support or community awareness, many of these properties are sold or allowed to fall into ruin.

- **Insufficient Government Support**: While there are some initiatives aimed at heritage conservation, government efforts are often insufficient and lack proper funding. There is a need for greater investment in heritage tourism, with an emphasis on restoration and community involvement to ensure the long-term sustainability of Mandawa's architectural treasures.

9.13 Socio-Economic Disparities

The economic benefits of tourism are not evenly distributed, leading to **socio-economic disparities** in Mandawa.

- **Economic Inequality**: While some sections of the population benefit from tourism (particularly hotel owners, guides, and shopkeepers), many others remain excluded from these benefits. The local economy remains largely **tourism-dependent**, which can be precarious and does not always provide stable, year-round employment.

- **Traditional Occupations Declining**: Traditional occupations, such as **craftsmanship** and **farming**, are declining due to the dominance of tourism. This has resulted in a loss of **skills** and **knowledge** associated with traditional arts and agriculture

10.CONCLUSION

Mandawa's architecture is not just a collection of buildings; it's a repository of history, art, culture, and social structure. The town stands as a witness to the prosperous past of Shekhawati, where wealthy merchants built opulent homes adorned with some of the finest frescoes in the world. However, much of this heritage is under threat, which is why efforts to preserve and restore Mandawa's architecture are crucial to keeping this "lost heritage" alive for future generations.

REFRENCES

- The Painted Towns of Shekhawati" by Ilay Cooper – A comprehensive book on the history, art, and architecture of Mandawa and other towns in the Shekhawati region.

- Tourism and Development in India: A Case Study" by Kevin Hannam – A broader discussion on the impact of tourism on small towns and heritage sites.

- Urban Development and Heritage Preservation in Rajasthan" – Research articles and studies that focus on the challenges of maintaining heritage in Rajasthan's historic towns.

ABOUT THE AUTHORS & EDITORS

Dr. Akshay Wayal (Ph.D. in Architecture) is presently working as an Assistant Professor at MIT ADT University, School of Architecture, Pune. He holds a PhD and Master's degree in Construction Management and a Bachelor's degree in Architecture. He has published research papers in various international journals and presented papers at national and international conferences. He is also appointed as a Board of Studies Member at PDEA's Prof. Ramkrishna More College, Pune, India for a Bachelor of Vocational Studies (B.Voc Interior Design).

Dr. Shobhan Sadhan Kelkar (Ph.D. in Architecture) is working as Professor and Head of The Department at STES' Smt. Kashibai Navale College of Architecture, Pune. She completed his Bachelor of Architecture (B.Arch), Master of Architecture (M.Arch in Architectural and Construction Project Management) and Ph.D. in Architecture. She has a vast academic experience of 24 years in the field of Architecture alomg with professional experience. For her Educational & Professional Experience and dedication in teaching she had been awarded for excellence in academics in 2021 at Architecture & Interior Design Excellence Awards at Bangalore and also Awarded 'Best Teacher' by Yashwant Vidyapeeth, Karad in 2015.

Dr. Ajinkya Pradeep Niphadkar is an Associate Professor with over 11 years of experience in the field of Architecture. He holds a PhD and Master's degree in Sustainable Architecture and a Bachelor's degree in Architecture. His areas of expertise include water conservation, energy-efficient materials, vernacular architecture, passive cooling techniques, and climate-responsive building designs.

Ajinkya has authored numerous research papers, focusing on tropical climates, building technology, and the integration of sustainable practices in residential and urban design. He has co-authored works on disaster management, affordable housing, and parametric design, and has contributed to several national and international conferences. His research also explores innovative teaching methods for architectural students, particularly for rural backgrounds and Marathi medium candidates.

.

www.ingramcontent.com/pod-product-compliance
Lightning Source LLC
Chambersburg PA
CBHW040907130726
48005CB00019BA/3015